THE PELICAN GUIDE TO

Plantation Homes of Louisiana

State of Louisiana Tour Map

THE PELICAN GUIDE TO

Plantation Homes
of Louisiana

EDITED BY ANNE BUTLER
PHOTOGRAPHS BY HENRY CANCIENNE

PELICAN PUBLISHING COMPANY
GRETNA 2009

First edition, May 1971
Second edition, August 1972
Third edition, May 1974
Fourth edition, August 1977
Fifth edition, January 1980
Sixth edition, January 1984
Second printing, September 1986
Seventh edition, January 1989
Eighth edition, April 2009

ISBN: 9781589806313

Printed in China
Published by Pelican Publishing Company, Inc.
1000 Burmaster Street, Gretna, Louisiana 70053

Contents

New Orleans to West Pointe a la Hache
(West Bank, Mississippi River)

THE FRENCH QUARTER
(A National Historic Landmark)

Merieult House
(OPEN TO PUBLIC)

Erected in 1792 during the Spanish colonial era by Jean François Merieult, this was one of the most elegant homes of its time and one of few structures surviving in the city after the disastrous fire of 1794. The

Merieult House

front of the house was remodeled in 1832, but the building was completely restored in the 1960s by inveterate collectors General and Mrs. L. Kemper Williams.

The structure now anchors The Historic New Orleans Collection, an outstanding house museum and research center interpreting state and local history and culture through changing exhibits and extensive collections of books, paintings, prints, maps, documents, and other significant artifacts.

Surrounding the courtyard are the Counting House and the Williams Residence, one of the Vieux Carré's "hidden houses," built in 1899 and adapted by noted architect Richard Koch to the needs and tastes of General and Mrs. Williams.

The Merieult House is listed on the National Register of Historic Places. The Historic New Orleans Collection is a member of the American Association of Museums.

Open Tuesday-Saturday 9:30-4:30; tours at 10, 11, 2, and 3. Entrance fee, except Williams Gallery free. Call (504) 523-4662. Online www.hnoc.org.

533 Royal St. in the French Quarter.

Marchand House

Built between 1808 and 1820, this restored French Quarter residence is constructed of brick with plaster and hand-hewn cypress.

Private.

830 Royal St. in the French Quarter.

Gallier House

Gallier House
(OPEN TO PUBLIC)

James Gallier, Jr., was one of New Orleans' most highly regarded 19th-century architects. His accomplishments include the impressive French Opera House and other notable structures, and when he put his considerable talents to work designing his own residence in 1857, the results were spectacular.

This comprehensive house museum, now a National Historic Landmark, has been carefully restored and filled with sumptuous furnishings of the 1860s, the period of Gallier's residency. Living-history demonstrations and seasonal changes in decor further enhance the interpretation of the past here.

Open Monday-Friday 10-4; last tour begins at 3; closed major holidays. Entrance fee. Call (504) 525-5661. Online www.hgghh.org.

1118 Royal St. in the French Quarter.

Hermann-Grima House

Hermann-Grima House
(OPEN TO PUBLIC)

One of the finest of French Quarter homes, the Hermann-Grima House was built in 1831 by wealthy merchant Samuel Hermann. A Federal mansion designed by William Brand, it has amazingly retained most of its original dependencies, including a horse stable, scullery, wine room, garçonnière, and even the cast-iron cistern at the rear of the beautifully landscaped courtyard.

The house has been painstakingly restored to accurately reflect the elegant lifestyle of prosperous Creole families in the Vieux Carré before the Civil War. Costumed docents discuss lifestyles, customs, and the decorative arts in these Golden Years of New Orleans, and lively special-focus tours and interpretive programs are conducted year round. In the functioning detached 1830s kitchen, open-hearth cooking demonstrations are given.

The Hermann-Grima House is a National Historic Landmark.

Open Monday-Friday 10-4; last tour begins at 3. Entrance fee. Call (504) 525-5661. Online www.hgghh.org.

820 St. Louis St. in the French Quarter.

Madame John's Legacy

Madame John's Legacy
(OPEN TO PUBLIC)

One of the oldest residences in New Orleans, Madame John's was neither a plantation home nor a palatial mansion, but its history is marked with mystery and links to Louisiana literature. Its name is derived from George Washington Cable's celebrated story "Tite Poulette," featuring Madame John, the quadroon mistress of the owner.

The house was built around 1788 to replace an earlier structure destroyed in the great fire that swept the city that year. Its builder was an American, Robert Jones, and it was the residence of Don Manuel de Lanzos, captain of the Spanish army in New Orleans. Though constructed during the Spanish colonial era, its design is typically French colonial, with living quarters raised above a brick basement said to have served as storage for contraband and a rendezvous for early pirates. One of Jean Lafitte's celebrated Baratarians, Renato Beluche who fought in the Battle of New Orleans, was born in this house.

The house was donated to the Louisiana State Museum in 1947 by Stella H. Lemann and is a National Historic Landmark.

Open Tuesday-Sunday 9-5. Entrance fee. Children under 12 free. Call (504) 568-6968. Online www.lsm.crt.state.la.us.

632 Dumaine St. in the French Quarter.

1850 House
(OPEN TO PUBLIC)

Located in a portion of the magnificent Pontalba Buildings facing Jackson Square in the French Quarter, the 1850 House re-creates a typical New Orleans dwelling of the period. Its splendid antique furnishings include pieces by Seignouret and Mallard, two of New Orleans' most famous cabinetmakers.

The two Pontalba rowhouse buildings, considered the oldest apartments in the United States, were constructed between 1849 and 1851 by Baroness Micaela Almonester de Pontalba. The 1850 House, in the Lower Pontalba Building, is a Louisiana State Museum and National Historic Landmark.

Open Tuesday-Saturday 9-5. Entrance fee. Call (504) 568-6968. Online www.lsm.crt.state.la.us.

525 St. Ann St. in the French Quarter.

1850 House

Beauregard-Keyes House
(OPEN TO PUBLIC)

This superbly simple Greek Revival cottage, built in 1826 by auctioneer Joseph LeCarpentier, takes its name from its two most famous occupants: Confederate general Pierre Gustave Toutant Beauregard and Frances Parkinson Keyes. Mrs. Keyes, celebrated author of more than 50 novels, lived in the house and created the Keyes Foundation to preserve and manage the property.

The raised cottage with its peaceful rear courtyard and lovely little side parterre garden displays a pronounced Federal influence, distinguishing it from most Vieux Carré dwellings.

The Beauregard-Keyes House, opposite the old Ursuline Convent, is listed on the National Register of Historic Places.

Open Monday-Saturday 10-3. Entrance fee. Call (504) 523-7257.

1113 Chartres St. in the French Quarter.

Beauregard-Keyes House

Lombard Plantation

This beautifully restored old structure is considered one of the last remaining examples of a Creole manor house. It was built in 1826 by Joseph Lombard, Sr., for his son and daughter-in-law. At that time the property included a large area adjacent to the Vieux Carré, which was later divided and sold. The interesting art nouveau brackets now on the gallery are an 1890s addition.
Private.
3933 Chartres St., east (downriver) of the French Quarter.

BAYOU SAINT JOHN

Louis Blanc House

This West Indian-style home built in 1798 has broad galleries and a large roof typical of New Orleans Spanish colonial architecture. The site was once part of the Bayou St. John properties of Don Almonester y Roxas, who sold it in 1793 to Louis Blanc, who in turn sold it to his son in 1816. A sketch by Charles Alexander Le Sueur about 1830 indicates that the house may then have been a one-story structure with gabled ends.
Private.
924 Moss St. on Bayou St. John.

De Matteo House

Although popularly known as the Old Spanish Custom House, there is no evidence that this structure ever was used for such a purpose. The land on which the house stands was purchased in 1771 by Juan Renato Huchet de Kernion, and the fine West Indies-style house may have been built in 1784, when the site was the plantation of Don Santiago Lloreins.
Private.
1300 Moss St. on Bayou St. John.

Holy Rosary Rectory

Holy Rosary Rectory

This building, also known as the Evariste Blanc House, was built about 1834 and was donated by Blanc's descendents for use as a parish church, parsonage, and school. Notable features include its fence, entrance doors, columns, dormers, and graceful balustrade of the captain's walk atop the roof. Side galleries are supported from the roof by iron rods instead of columns, as on the front. The five Ionic columns of the entrance doorways and other details from the 1830s indicate the Greek Revival influence. It is now the rectory of Our Lady of the Holy Rosary Church.
Private.
1342 Moss St. on Bayou St. John.

Morel-Wisner House

This 1850s Greek Revival raised cottage, possibly constructed as a residence for attorney Christoval Morel, housed in 1882 the first fencing club in New Orleans and also served as headquarters of a famous rowing club.
Private.
1347 Moss St. on Bayou St. John.

Pitot House

Pitot House
(OPEN TO PUBLIC)

Listed on the National Register of Historic Places, Pitot House has been beautifully restored by the Louisiana Landmarks Society.

Built about 1799 and purchased in 1810 by James Pitot, the first elected mayor of incorporated New Orleans after the Louisiana Purchase, this Creole colonial house was moved from its original nearby location in 1964.

Open Wednesday-Saturday 10-3; closed holidays. Entrance fee. Call (504) 482-0312. Online www.louisianalandmarks.org.

1440 Moss St. on Bayou St. John.

Wilkinson Home

This fine Greek Revival house was once the property of Evariste Blanc. Blanc purchased the property from the succession of Etienne Reine in 1847, and the present house was constructed some time after that date.

The Robert Musgrove family owned it from 1859 until 1882.

Private.

1454 Moss St. on Bayou St. John.

THE GARDEN DISTRICT
(A National Historic Landmark)

Westfeldt House

This square, raised cottage was probably built circa 1838 on the edge of the old Livaudais plantation, which was purchased in 1832 for $490,000 from Madame Jacques François Livaudais, then living in Paris, and subdivided to become the picturesque section known as the Garden District. The property was laid out to resemble a huge park and was filled with the classic mansions built by the Americans who poured into the area after the Louisiana Purchase of 1803. They settled in the Garden District in order to remove themselves from the French and Spanish colonial influences of the older Creole section of the city, the Vieux Carré.

New Orleans is a city eternally in bloom, with an enormous variety of flora thriving in its warm, humid climate and fertile, alluvial soil, and nowhere is this better seen than along the oak-shaded avenues of the Garden District. The fine gardens set off elaborately furnished homes built mostly from the 1840s through the 1860s in a communal display of newly acquired Anglo-American wealth.

One of the oldest homes in the Garden District, the Westfeldt House was extensively altered in 1855. A beautiful live oak on the grounds is a frequent subject for artists.

Private.

2340 Prytania St.

Westfeldt House

The Jacob Payne-Strachan House

The Jacob Payne-Strachan House

On December 6, 1889, this classic 1849 Greek Revival home, with five bays and double galleries, was the scene of Jefferson Davis's death. When the president of the Confederacy fell ill, he had been brought to the home of his friend Judge Charles Fenner, son-in-law of homeowner Jacob Payne.

Private.

1134 First St.

The Brevard-Rice House

An 1857 Greek Revival structure later decorated with an Italianate bay, this three-story residence has an ornate two-level columned entry porch and inside, double parlors separated by an elliptical archway.

It was designed by architect James Calrow for Albert Brevard but is best known for a later resident, author Anne Rice, who used it in her novel *The Witching Hour* as the ancestral home of the Mayfair witches. (Rice locates the Mayfair family tomb in nearby Lafayette Cemetery No. 1, one of New Orleans' "cities of the dead" with its unique above-ground tombs. The cemetery dates from 1833 and is entered just across from world-famous Commander's Palace restaurant).

Private.

1239 First St.

Brevard-Rice House

The Walter Robinson House

Built beginning in 1859 for Virginian Walter Robinson, whose wealth came from tobacco and banking, this center-hall house had a roof designed to collect water, providing rare early indoor plumbing.

With its striking appearance and perfection of scale, this home is considered the masterpiece of Irish-born architect Henry Howard, who lived on First Street and designed at least two dozen homes in the Garden District, as well as many plantation manors in outlying areas. The 80-block Garden District, now a National Historic Landmark as well as a National Register of Historic Places district bordered by Josephine St., Magazine St., Louisiana Ave., and Carondelet St., boasts prime examples of the works of the best builders and architects in Crescent City history, including Howard, James Gallier, Jr., and Paris-trained William A. Freret.

Private.

1415 Third St.

Walter Robinson House

Cornstalk fence surrounding the Robert Short House

The Robert Short House

Designed by noted architect Henry Howard, this fine home was built for a cost of about $24,000 and is most noted for its famous cornstalk fence. One explanation for the fence's unusual design was that the wife of first owner Col. Robert Short was homesick for the Iowa cornfields where she had grown up.

Private.

1448 Fourth St.

Audubon Park

This beautiful 247-acre park now stands on what once were the Foucher and de Boré plantations, the latter distinguished by the fact that its owner first granulated sugar commercially there in 1795. In 1884 the area was the site of the World's Industrial and Cotton Centennial Exposition. The master plan for the park was designed by John Charles Olmstead in 1897. A statue of naturalist John James Audubon may be seen, as well as gardens, an amusement center, and the expansive zoo.

St. Charles Ave., across from Tulane University.

WEST BANK

Aurora

More than a century old, Aurora has round columns supporting a gallery across the front. The roof is supported by slender colonnettes that rise from the second-floor gallery.

Private.

Patterson Dr. in the Aurora Gardens section of Algiers, west bank of the Mississippi River.

Woodland Plantation

(OPEN TO PUBLIC)

The last plantation left standing in the Deep Delta on the Mississippi River's west bank, the property dates back to 1834 when William Johnson was a prosperous sugar baron and river pilot. His son Bradish was said to have worn a tall silk hat, Prince Albert coat, and striped pants everyday. During Prohibition, bootleggers found safe haven here.

Extensive grounds along the river batture include an overseer's house, slave cabin, and 1880s chapel with vaulted ceiling and stained-glass windows ideal for weddings, receptions, group meals, and retreats. Fishing expeditions can be planned, and overnight accommodations are provided in the main house, which appears on the label of Southern Comfort.

Call (504) 656-9990. Online www.woodlandplantation.com.

21997 La. Hwy. 23, two miles above West Pointe a la Hache.

Woodland Plantation

TOUR 2
Pointe a la Hache to New Orleans
(East Bank, Mississippi River)

Promised Land

The original section of this home probably dates from the early 18th century and has hand-hewn beams joined with wooden pegs.
Private.
La. Hwy. 39 (River Rd.), below Dalcour.

Mary

Authentically restored to its original West Indies design, with double galleries and exterior stairs, the house dates from the 18th century.
Private.
La. Hwy. 39 (River Rd.), at Dalcour.

Stella

A 19th-century brick and cypress raised cottage, Stella's hand-hewn shingled roof overhangs the front gallery, supported by six columns. The grounds are lush with citrus trees.
Private.
La. Hwy. 39 (River Rd.), six miles below Braithwaite.

Kenilworth

Originally a one-story Spanish block-house built in 1759, Kenilworth gained a second floor shortly after 1800. Its wide galleries are supported by massive brick columns, and the roof by cypress colonnettes. On land owned by the Bienvenue and Estopinal families, it was frequented by General Beauregard, and family lore mentions ghosts.
Private; open by appointment only.
2931 La. Hwy. 46 (Bayou Rd.), St. Bernard.

Sebastopol Plantation

A careful restoration has restored the Creole roots of this 1830s home built by Pierre Marin and Evariste Wagan. It was named in honor of the impressive Russian defeat of the Crimean War.

This plantation is listed on the National Register of Historic Places.

Private; open by appointment only.

721 La. Hwy. 46 (Bayou Rd.), St. Bernard.

Pecan Grove Plantation

A sugar plantation dating to the time of the Battle of New Orleans, it is now filled with historic artifacts.

Private; open by appointment only.

10 Pecan Grove, Meraux.

Pecan Grove Plantation

Malus-Beauregard House
(OPEN TO PUBLIC)

Built in the 1830s, this home was once occupied by Judge Rene Beauregard, son of the Confederate general. The building is of cement-covered brick and has two stories and an attic. Supported by eight Doric columns, wide upper and lower galleries extend along the front and rear of the home. The house was remodeled in 1856 and again in 1865, both remodelings attributed to noted architect James Gallier, Jr.

The building was restored in 1957 and again after Hurricanes Katrina and Rita flooded the structure and severely damaged the surrounding trees. Overlooking the banks of the Mississippi River, the house is on the Chalmette Battlefield, part of the Jean Lafitte National Historical Park and the site of Andrew Jackson's stunning victory over the British in the Battle of New Orleans. A 1.5-mile tour route includes interpretive visitor center, monolithic monument, authentic cannon, and reconstructed rampart. Chalmette National Cemetery, begun in 1864, is adjacent to the house site.

Open daily 9-5. Free. Call (504) 589-3882. Online www.nps.gov/jela.

La. Hwy. 46 (St. Bernard Hwy.), six miles below New Orleans.

Malus-Beauregard House

TOUR 3

New Orleans to Baton Rouge
(East Bank, Mississippi River)

Whitehall/Magnolia School

Built about 1850 by François Pascalis de Labarre, this classical style raised villa is fronted by a wide, columned gallery and set in a grove of magnolias, cedars, and live oaks. During the Civil War, Federal troops camped here. The home remained in the Labarre family until 1892, then was converted into a gambling house and later a Jesuit retreat. Since 1935, Whitehall has served as a boarding school for special-needs children. It is now called Magnolia School. 100 Central Ave. at U.S. Hwy. 90 (River Rd.), Jefferson, across from New Orleans.

LaBranche Plantation Dependency
(OPEN TO PUBLIC)

The long-gone main house of LaBranche Plantation was built in the 1790s by members of the Zweig family along what was called the German Coast for its large numbers of early Teutonic settlers. Zweig, German for "twig" or "branch," was anglicized over the years.

What remains of the plantation is the picturesque dependency known as the garçonniere, where adolescent boys of the family were housed.

Assorted items of interest here include Zachary Taylor's bathtub, a slave dwelling, and the grave of Hitler's horse Nordlicht, sire of a number of Louisiana racehorses.

LaBranche is listed on the National Register of Historic Places.

Open for tours weekends 9:30-4. Entrance fee. Call (504) 468-8843. La. Hwy. 48 (River Rd.), St. Rose.

Destrehan Plantation
(OPEN TO PUBLIC)

The oldest documented plantation home in the lower Mississippi Valley, Destrehan was built in 1787 by a free mulatto named Charles Paquet for Robin de Logny and was acquired by de Logny's son-in-law Jean Noel Destrehan in 1792. The plantation, whose early owners were French nobility, at one time encompassed 6,000 acres of indigo and then sugarcane. It was Destrehan's brother-in-law Etienne de Boré, first mayor of New Orleans, who perfected the granulation of sugar.

Near the close of the Civil War, the house was seized by the Union army and used by the Freedmen's Bureau to teach trades to newly freed slaves. After a period of 20th-century industrial ownership, it was donated by Amoco to the nonprofit River Road Historical Society, which has done a remarkable job restoring and appropriately furnishing the home.

The two wings are 1810 additions to the original building, which in 1840 was remodeled in the Greek Revival style while retaining its uncommon West Indies roof. Inside, exposed lathing walls, openings into the pegged attic, and bousillage still bearing fingerprints of its original creators provide a rare look at early building techniques, while living-history demonstrations by costumed artisans demonstrate the requisite skills of early plantation life.

Destrehan is on the National Register of Historic Places.

Open daily 9-4; closed holidays. Entrance fee. Call (985) 764-9315. Online www.destrehanplantation.org.

13034 La. Hwy. 48 (River Rd.), at Destrehan.

Destrehan Plantation

Ormond Plantation

Ormond Plantation
(OPEN FOR WEDDINGS)

A two-story French West Indies-style structure of briquette-entre-poteaux (slave-made bricks between cypress studs), this home predates the 1790s. Two flanking garçonniers are connected to the main section by upper galleries.

The earliest owner was Pierre d'Trepagnier, who grew indigo and then sugarcane on lands granted him by Spanish governor Galvez. Summoned from the dinner table by a servant to meet a Spanish gentleman in 1798, d'Trepagnier disappeared without a trace.

His property was purchased in 1805 by Col. Richard Butler, descendent of Revolutionary War heroes, who named it Ormond after his ancestral Irish castle. Butler died of yellow fever at age 43, and a later owner, Basile LaPlace, Jr., who supposedly had made enemies in state politics, was in his turn called out into the night. His body, riddled with bullets, was hanged from one of the large live oaks on the grounds. Is it any wonder Ormond has more than its share of ghost stories?

Open for weddings. Call (985) 764-8544.

13786 La. Hwy. 48 (River Rd.), Destrehan.

San Francisco Plantation

(OPEN TO PUBLIC)

This magnificent structure, a landmark along the Mississippi River, was built in the early 1850s by Edmond Bozonier Marmillion and lavishly and expensively redecorated by his son Valsin, who subsequently dubbed it "St. Frusquin" (from the local patois *sans fruscins,* meaning without a penny in my pocket).

Resplendent with scrolls, fluted pillars, rococo grillwork, and galleries reminiscent of some of the more ornate riverboats, San Francisco's design, while actually French in style, is often called "Steamboat Gothic," which inspired both the name and the setting of a novel by Frances Parkinson Keyes.

Owned and operated by the nonprofit San Francisco Plantation Foundation, subsidized by Marathon Oil, the house has been elaborately furnished and authentically restored to its original splendor, complete with fine faux bois and faux marble finishes, hand-painted ceiling frescoes, and a vivid Victorian palette inside and out, including the flanking cisterns of brilliant blue capped by unique Moorish metal domes.

San Francisco Plantation is a National Historic Landmark.

Tours daily 9:40-4:40 (last tour 4, November-March); closed holidays. Entrance fee. Call (985) 535-2341. Online www.sanfranciscoplantation.org. 2646 La. Hwy. 44 (River Rd.), Garyville.

San Francisco Plantation

Graugnard House

This last surviving structure from Terre Haute Plantation was the turn-of-the-century home of planter Leon Graugnard. It is listed on the National Register of Historic Places.

Private.

On La. Hwy. 44 (River Rd.), Reserve.

Manresa House of Retreats/Jefferson College

This elongated three-story Greek Revival structure features 22 columns in an unbroken row across its main facade and a triangular pediment above the central section. A magnificent oak alley connects it to the river.

Built in 1831 as nonsectarian Jefferson College for the higher education of the sons of wealthy Louisiana planters, it closed in 1848 and was reopened as Louisiana College. Wealthy planter Valcour Aime purchased the site in 1859 and erected a chapel in memory of his children.

During the Civil War, the building was used as a barracks by the Union forces. In 1864, Aime donated it to the Roman Catholic Marist Fathers, who operated it as St. Mary's Jefferson College. On the National Register of Historic Places, it now belongs to the Jesuit Order who operate the property as the Manresa House of Retreats.

Private.

La. Hwy. 44 (River Rd.), two miles south of Convent.

Judge Felix Poché Plantation

(OPEN TO PUBLIC)

A Victorian Renaissance Revival plantation house built just prior to 1870, this home was originally owned by Judge Felix Pierre Poché, political leader and prominent jurist. The judge was a state supreme court justice and was called one of the founders of the American Bar Association. His scholarly diaries of Civil War times were written in impeccable French.

Now a bed and breakfast, the home is on the National Register of Historic Places.

Open daily 10-5; overnight accommodations and RV hook-up service. Entrance fee. Call (225) 562-7728. Online www.pocheplantation.com.

6554 La. Hwy. 44 (River Rd.), Convent.

Malarcher House

Malarcher House

Le Chevalier Louis Malarcher, a political refugee from the French Revolution, became a prominent leader in St. James Parish and built the original house here. When it was destroyed in 1890 at the time of the levee break through the Nita Crevasse just to the north, his grandson built the present Creole cottage on the site.

Private.

La. Hwy. 44 (River Rd.), just north of Poché Plantation, Convent.

Uncle Sam Plantation Site

Once one of the area's most efficient and spectacular plantation communities, Uncle Sam had seven large buildings and 40 smaller ones. The largest was the main house, 100 feet square not counting the broad surrounding galleries. It was a two-storied structure of plastered brick with a dormered hip roof supported on all sides by 28 giant Doric columns. It was said to have cost $100,000 to build and an additional $75,000 to furnish.

Originally known as Constancia, the plantation took its lasting name from owner Samuel Fagot, who erected the mansion between 1837 and 1843; his friends and family fondly called him "Uncle Sam."

The buildings and plantation were demolished in 1940 to make way for levee construction to prevent further land erosion by the river. The site is now industrial.

La. Hwy. 44 (River Rd.), one and a half miles north of Convent.

Tezcuco Plantation Ruins

Tezcuco Plantation

Monument to past glories and the tragic fate awaiting far too many fragile historic properties, Tezcuco's site is marked solely by brick chimneys rising starkly to the sky beneath the towering live oaks. The 1850s house was built for Mexican War veteran Benjamin Tureaud, who named it for the lake near Mexico City where Montezuma fled the Spanish conquistador Cortez. Tezcuco means "resting place" in Aztec.

The large raised cottage, 4,500 square feet with 15-foot ceilings and ornate gallery grillwork of iron, was toured by thousands and was also a popular bed and breakfast and restaurant until it burned completely to the ground in May 2002.

3138 La. Hwy. 44 (River Rd.), Darrow.

Houmas House
(OPEN TO PUBLIC)

It is called the Sugar Palace, and indeed this glorious Greek Revival mansion has been associated with some of the most prominent planters of the south—Revolutionary War hero Wade Hampton, who was the state's largest sugar producer when he began the plantation in the early 1800s; his architect son-in-law Col. John Smith Preston, who finished the house in the 1840s; and just prior to the Civil War, John Burnside, who boasted over 300,000 acres planted in sugarcane and as a British subject saved the house from destruction during the Civil War with claims of neutrality.

But before that, the land was the site of a Houma Indian village surrounded by vast herds of bison when Alexandre Latil in the 1770s began building the two-story brick dogtrot structure presently called the French House. This simple early building houses the open-hearth kitchen and is now connected at the upper level to the rear of the main house, forming a shady carriageway at ground level.

Today, Houmas House stands as one of the most imposing of Louisiana's fabled antebellum structures: two and a half stories, with 14 columns across the front and sides, crowned by arched dormers and a glass-windowed belvedere, and flanked by hexagonal garçonnieres.

Inside are magnificent period furnishings by the 19th century's most notable craftsmen, extensive collections of fine art, and an impressive three-story spiral staircase. Outside on the 32-acre grounds, centuries-old oaks and magnolias shade lush tropical plantings, ponds, and fountains, with inviting pathways and playful statuary at every turn.

The late Dr. George Crozat accomplished a superb restoration of Houmas House when he bought it in 1940, a century after it was completed, and more recently, devoted owner Kevin Kelly has worked his own miracles.

Hush, Hush, Sweet Charlotte was filmed here.

Houmas House is listed on the National Register of Historic Places.

Open for tours Monday-Tuesday 9-5, Wednesday-Sunday 9-8. Entrance fee. Weddings and events. Restaurants. Call (225) 473-7841. Online www.houmashouse.com.

40136 La. Hwy. 942 (River Rd.), Burnside. Accessible from I-10 via Burnside exit #179.

Houmas House

Bocage
(OPEN TO PUBLIC)

This two-story home featuring 18-inch-thick brick walls below and wood above is square in appearance and classic in design. The front gallery features an unusual arrangement of wooden pillars, the outer six large square ones and the central pair, thin and light in contrast. Greek Revival in design, Bocage is comparatively small at 7,400 square feet, including galleries. A heavy entablature hides the roof.

This finely ornamented gem, with marble floors downstairs, was built in 1801 by Emanuel Marius Pons Bringier as a present for his 15-year-old daughter, Francoise, upon the occasion of her marriage to Christophe Colomb, a Parisian who claimed kinship with Christopher Columbus.

Bocage—which means "shady retreat" in French—was one of the showplaces along the Mississippi River around the time of the Civil War. New ownership has meant extensive long-term restoration and the possibility for future public access with plans for tours, restaurants, and events. It is listed on the National Register of Historic Places.

Online www.lebocage.com.

La. Hwy. 942 (River Rd.), two miles above Burnside.

Bocage

L'Hermitage
(OPEN TO PUBLIC)

With original walls of brick-between-posts and surrounded by 24 Doric Tuscan columns and wide double galleries, L'Hermitage is a splendid structure of massive simplicity, surely one of the earliest surviving Greek Revival plantation homes in Louisiana.

It was built in the early 1800s by Marius Pons Bringier and first leased and then transferred to his son, Michel Douradou, after his marriage to Louise Elizabeth Aglae duBourg de St. Colomb. Indigo was the cash crop here until at least 1812.

The Bringier men were among the Creoles who fought under Gen. Andrew Jackson in the War of 1812. Douradou named L'Hermitage after the Tennessee home of his hero, who visited after the Battle of New Orleans.

The Robert Judices, long active in historical groups and owners for the last half-century, have been recognized with preservation awards for their sensitive restoration of L'Hermitage. It is listed on the National Register of Historic Places.

Open daily. Call (225) 473-3996.

38308 La. Hwy. 942 (River Rd.), Darrow.

L'Hermitage

Ashland/Belle Helene

A huge Greek Revival house of unusual height and restrained elegance, Ashland is surrounded by eight 30-foot-tall giant square pillars on each side and is topped by a full heavy entablature. Galleries extend nearly 20 feet on each side.

Built in 1841 for Duncan Farrar Kenner, a wealthy politician and attorney who served as Confederate minister plenipotentiary to France and England, the structure was named after Henry Clay's home. Ashland was designed by prominent New Orleans architect James Gallier, Sr., as a wedding gift from Kenner to his wife, Nanine Bringier. Besides being a great statesman, Kenner was also a widely respected planter, and Ashland was one of the great sugar plantations.

Subsequent owner John B. Reuss renamed the plantation Belle Helene for his granddaughter, Helene. Now it is owned by Shell Chemical Company.

Scenes for Warner Brothers' motion picture *Band of Angels,* starring Clark Gable, were filmed here in 1957, and *Beguiled,* starring Clint Eastwood and Geraldine Page, was made here in 1970.

Ashland is listed on the National Register of Historic Places.

Private.

La. Hwy. 75 (River Rd.), six miles above Darrow.

Ashland/Belle Helene

Indian Camp Plantation
(OPEN TO PUBLIC)

Architect Henry Howard designed this graceful Greek Revival house in the late 1850s for sugarcane planter Robert Coleman Camp. The house departs from the characteristic Louisiana raised cottage with the extension of two recessed symmetrical wings with upper balconies. The central portion of the house is supported by six square brick columns that meet six Corinthian columns to support the roof of the structure.

In 1894, Dr. Isadore Dyer, dean of Tulane University's medical school, established a state hospital for the treatment of leprosy at Indian Camp, having run into such public opposition in other locations that he initially leased the site under pretence of opening an ostrich farm and had to transport the first patients upriver on a coal barge when all other vessels refused to accept them as passengers.

The U.S. Public Health Service operated the national leprosarium, later known as the Gillis Long Hansen's Disease Center, on the site beginning in 1921. In 1999 the property returned to state ownership when the hospital relocated its operations and most of its patients (a few opted to stay). The hospital property now houses National Guard operations, with the plantation house as administrative building.

The National Hansen's Disease Museum through touching exhibits interprets the battle against this most dread and misunderstood disease by determined doctors, brave nurses of the Daughters of Charity, and resident patients, many of whom were quarantined for life.

The plantation house and hospital complex are listed on the National Register of Historic Places.

Museum open Tuesday-Saturday 10-4; closed holidays. Walking tour last Saturday afternoon of each month. Call (225) 642-1950. Online www.hrsa.gov/hansens/museum/default.htm.

5445 Point Clair Rd., Carville.

Longwood

Built during the Spanish occupation, Longwood is a cypress building with a hipped roof supported by slender wooden columns. Both of its galleries have iron railings. The back part of the house was added to the present structure in 1835.

Private.

La. Hwy. 327-991 (River Rd.), 10 miles south of Baton Rouge.

LSU Rural Life Museum
(OPEN TO PUBLIC)

Located on the Burden Research Plantation, a 450-acre agricultural research experiment station owned by Louisiana State University, the Rural Life Museum preserves an important part of the state's heritage. Conceived and developed by Steele and Ione Burden and Cecil G. Taylor, former chancellor of LSU in Baton Rouge, the museum encompasses five acres and more than 25 buildings and features hundreds of artifacts reflecting plantation life in 18th- and 19th-century Louisiana. The museum is divided into three areas: the Barn, the Working Plantation, and Louisiana Folk Architecture.

Structures range from a tiny dovecote and four-hole outhouse to a church, syrup house with sugarcane grinder, slave quarters, Acadian cottage, commissary, and jail, comprising the largest collection of historic material culture in the state. Some of the buildings are original period structures illustrative of the influence of the varying ethnic and cultural backgrounds of their builders, and they are authentically equipped with vintage tools, household utensils, furniture, and farm implements.

The Barn's fascinating exhibits focus on such significant subjects as slavery, medicine, logging, woodcrafts, Native Americans, textiles, religion, fishing, and hunting and trapping.

Adjacent to the museum are the lovely 25-acre Windrush Gardens, thoughtfully planned and planted by Steele Burden, who was a widely respected landscape designer, and the Burden House, which is private.

Open daily 8:30-5; closed holidays. Advance registration required for groups. Entrance fee. Call (225) 765-2437. Online http://rurallife.lsu.edu. 4650 Essen Ln., just south of I-10 intersection, Baton Rouge.

Mount Hope Plantation
(OPEN TO PUBLIC)

Built on a Spanish land grant obtained in 1786, Mount Hope was constructed in 1817 by Joseph Sharp, a German planter. One of the Baton Rouge area's last remaining 19th-century farmhouses, the beautifully furnished Greek Revival structure has 12.5-foot ceilings typical of early southern planters' efforts to make life bearable in hot, humid summers.

This imposing home, which hosted an encampment of Confederate troops during the Civil War, is listed on the National Register of Historic Places.

Open for weddings, receptions, overnight accommodations. Call (225) 761-7000. Online www.nps.gov/history/nr/travel/louisiana/mou.htm. 8151 Highland Rd., Baton Rouge.

Magnolia Mound Plantation

Magnolia Mound Plantation
(OPEN TO PUBLIC)

This fine French Creole home, built around 1791 of cypress beams with bousillage-entre-poteau insulation, has a front porch 80 feet long. It was once the home of Prince Achille Murat, son of Charles Louis Napoleon Achille Murat, and nephew of Bonaparte and the Crown Prince of Naples. The original simple structure was enlarged after 1802 by Armand Duplantier.

The house, which took its name from its grove of trees, was sensibly built on a bluff, or mound, overlooking the Mississippi to catch the cooling breezes from the river.

The structure looks very much as it did in the early 19th century. Wide, single-storied, and built almost five feet off the ground, it boasts beautifully preserved hand-carved woodwork and thick cypress plank floors. Exquisite furnishings are mostly Federal period, many of them made in Louisiana.

Magnolia Mound is listed on the National Register of Historic Places and its Historic House Museum is accredited by the American Association of Museums. Almost lost to urban development, the home was saved in the nick of time and is now the well-run property of the Recreation and Park Commission of East Baton Rouge Parish (BREC).

Special living-history demonstrations and hands-on learning activities are offered for students with advance arrangement.

On the 16-acre grounds are kitchen and cash crop gardens, pigeonnier, overseer's house and slave quarter house. The reconstructed outside kitchen is the setting for open-hearth cooking.

Open Monday-Saturday 10-4, Sunday 1-4; tours on the hour, with last tour at 3. Weddings and events. Entrance fee. Call (225) 343-4955. Online www.magnoliamound.org.

2161 Nicholson Dr., Baton Rouge.

Stewart-Dougherty House

This imposing two-story home was built for Nathan Knox by master craftsman Nelson Potts in the late 1840s. Massive square plastered-brick columns with recessed paneling support a hipped roof and second-floor gallery railed with iron grillwork.

Shortly after the house was built, it was purchased by Mrs. Nolan Stewart, daughter of pioneer landowner James McCalop, and for many years afterward it was maintained by her descendents.

In 1862 and 1863, during the Civil War, it was used as a U.S. general hospital.

The Stewart-Dougherty House is listed on the National Register of Historic Places.

Private.

741 North St., Baton Rouge.

Potts House

This two-story brick townhouse in Spanish Town, the oldest neighborhood in the city of Baton Rouge, was built in 1846 by Nelson Potts, formerly of New Jersey. An accomplished brick mason, Potts established a brickyard on the outskirts of town. It is likely that he built his family home at the edge of the brickyard as a prime example of his fine handicraft. Over time, he would do the brickwork for many local structures, both private residences and public institutions, as well as sidewalks, cisterns, and walls.

Potts House, of Greek Revival design and enhanced by plantings of tropical palms, is listed on the National Register of Historic Places.

Private.

831 North St., Baton Rouge.

Goodwood

This impressive home was built of cement-covered brick in 1856 by Dr. S. G. Laycock on land granted to Thomas Hutchings by George III in 1776. It has broad, iron-railed galleries supported by four Doric columns across the front. Goodwood had running water piped to washstands in all rooms, an unusual feature for a home of the time.

Private.

7307 Goodwood Ave. at Lobdell Ave., Baton Rouge.

TOUR 4

Baton Rouge to New Orleans
(West Bank, Mississippi River)

Poplar Grove
(OPEN TO PUBLIC)

Listed on the National Register of Historic Places, Poplar Grove was built as an Oriental-inspired pavilion designed by architect Thomas Sully for the 1884 World's Industrial and Cotton Centennial Exposition in New Orleans. It was moved 200 miles upriver by barge to house generations of the Wilkinson family, successful sugar planters and descendants of Gen. James Wilkinson. Open by appointment for tours, dinners, and weddings. Call (225) 344-3913. Online www.poplargroveplantation.com. 3142 North River Rd., Port Allen.

Monte Vista
Begun in 1857 by Louis Favrot, this classical home has had a long association with the Wilkinson family, descended from Gen. James Wilkinson. In 1803, Wilkinson and Gov. W. C. C. Claiborne, received the Louisiana Territory for the U.S. It is on the National Register of Historic Places.
Private.
La. Hwy. 1 (River Rd.), Port Allen.

St. Louis
St. Louis, listed on the National Register of Historic Places, is a Greek Revival structure with six Ionic columns supporting the first gallery and six more ornate Corinthian ones up top. With a rooftop belvedere and rich cast-iron work, the house with its rare cellar was built in 1858 by Edward J. Gay of St. Louis, who named it after that city. It was called Home Plantation when established by Capt. Joseph Erwin in 1807.
Private.
La. Hwy. 405 (River Rd.), just south of Plaquemine.

Tallyho Plantation

Tallyho Plantation

Originally the overseer's home, this building was occupied by the owners when the main house burned. Built about 1840, the house is a provincial Greek Revival plantation home featuring Doric pillars with molded capitals. Tallyho has been in the Murrell family for well over a century.
Tallyho is on the National Register of Historic Places.
Private.
La. Hwy. 405 (River Rd.), just south of Bayou Goula.

Mulberry Grove

A classic double-galleried Greek Revival structure built in 1836 by Dr. Edward Duffel, Mulberry Grove was in use as a hay barn in the 1950s, when it was reclaimed and restored.
Private.
La. Hwy. 405 (River Rd.), seven miles below White Castle.

Nottoway Plantation

Nottoway Plantation
(OPEN TO PUBLIC)

The largest antebellum plantation home in the south, Nottoway is an unusual three-story mansion with 64 rooms under its slate roof. At 53,000 square feet, it was considered immense even by the standards of the antebellum "Golden Age."

Henry Howard, noted New Orleans architect, was commissioned by John Hampden Randolph to build this palatial residence, which blends Greek Revival and Italianate architectural styles. Completed in 1859 and named for the Virginia county of Mr. Randolph's birth, Nottoway was the center of a self-sufficient 7,000-acre sugarcane plantation.

The home's beautifully furnished interior features an entrance hall 20 feet wide, seven inside stairways, 16 fireplaces, 200 windows, and 365 doors. Its ceilings are 15.5 feet tall. Wings to the side and rear accommodated the 11 children of the family as well as the detached kitchen. A graceful curved side section holds the famous white ballroom with Corinthian columns supporting triple arches and elaborate plaster frieze work, all in glistening white.

Nottoway is listed on the National Register of Historic Places.

Open daily 9-5. Entrance fee. Restaurant. Overnight accommodations. Weddings and events. Call (225) 545-2730. Online www.nottoway.com. 30970 La. Hwy. 405 (River Rd.), White Castle.

Oak Alley Plantation

Oak Alley Plantation
(OPEN TO PUBLIC)

Magnificent Oak Alley was built in 1839 in the Greek Revival style and of plastered brick. Seventy feet square and girded by 28 Doric columns, each eight feet in circumference, it was built by French Creole sugar planter Jacques Telesphore Roman III, brother of Andre Bienvenu Roman, twice governor of Louisiana, and was originally called Bon Sejour.

Riverboat passengers awed by the double row of live oaks viewed when approaching the house from the river landing soon dubbed the place Oak Alley instead, and indeed the famed avenue of oaks is one of the most impressive in the south. Planted three centuries ago by some early French settler, no doubt, some of these trees measure as much as 30 feet around, their upper branches interlaced to form a leafy canopy from road to house. Spacing between the 28 venerable trees is exactly 80 feet.

The home was beautifully restored by the late Mr. and Mrs. Andrew Stewart, who furnished it with fine period pieces and established a non-profit foundation to assure its preservation.

Oak Alley is a National Historic Landmark.

Open daily 9-5:30 March-October; 9-5 November-February; closed holidays. Entrance fee. Overnight accommodations. Restaurant. Call (225) 265-2151. Online www.oakalleyplantation.com.

3645 La. Hwy. 18 (River Rd.), Vacherie.

St. Joseph Plantation
(OPEN TO PUBLIC)

With lower walls of brick 14 inches thick and the upper living quarters of briquette-entre-poteaux construction (moss and clay between cypress columns, under weatherboard walls), Creole-style St. Joseph was built about 1830, before Greek Revival architecture became the rage along the Great River Road. Ten large brick columns rise from the ground floor to the 90-foot-long gallery; above, 10 square wooden ones support the steep, hipped roof. Dozens of French doors and windows are carefully positioned to maximize cross-ventilation.

An early resident was Dr. Cazamine Mericq, one of Napoleon's royal surgeons. It was purchased from him by immensely wealthy sugar planter Valcour Aime as a wedding present for his daughter Josephine, who raised 10 children in the house. In 1877 the home and 1,000 acres were acquired at a sheriff's sale by Joseph Waguespack, who had come from Alsace-Lorraine to settle in this section of Louisiana, called the Côte des Allemands (German Coast), and his descendents have been raising sugarcane on the land ever since.

St. Joseph is on the National Register of Historic Places.

Open Monday-Saturday 9:30-5, Sunday from noon; last tour 4:30. Weddings. Call (225) 265-4078. Online www.stjosephplantation.com

3535 La. Hwy. 18 (River Rd.), Vacherie.

St. Joseph Plantation

Felicity

Built about 1850 by Valcour Aime as a wedding present for one of his daughters, Felicity has six large, square wooden pillars. For years the home was in the family of Joseph Waguespack, the same family who has owned St. Joseph since the 1870s.

Private.

La. Hwy. 18 (River Rd.), Vacherie.

Laura Plantation
(OPEN TO PUBLIC)

In startling contrast to the austere purity of the ubiquitous white-columned Greek Revival homes so beloved by the Anglo planters along the River Road sits this colorful Creole plantation house. With bright red roof, ochre walls, and green trim, Laura dates from 1805. The plantation's dozen historic structures vividly explore the culmination of Creole culture in the state, in between the fading of the French and Spanish regimes and the arrival of the adventurous Americans.

The 12,000-acre plantation began with French war hero Guillaume DuParc, who had his own sugar mill and nearly 200 slaves. Tours today center around the memoirs of his observant great-granddaughter Laura Locoul Gore, for whom the plantation was named, and also the African folktales told by early Senegalese slaves here and considered the precursors of the beloved B'rer Rabbit stories of Uncle Remus.

Laura Plantation

Laura stands as striking testament to the resilience of historic properties and the determination of those who love them. Deteriorating and sold at auction, wrecked by hurricanes and nearly destroyed by devastating fires, Laura has endured, thanks most especially to the dedicated and continuing struggles of Norm and Sand Marmillion, whose research efforts not only uncovered the memoirs of Laura Locoul but also unearthed hundreds of related documents in the French national archives, forming the basis of fascinating interpretive tours here.

Laura is listed on the National Register of Historic Places.

Open daily 10-4; closed holidays. Call (225) 265-7690. Online www.lauraplantation.com.

2247 La. Hwy. 18 (River Rd.), Vacherie.

Whitney Plantation

A dedicated, decade-long restoration effort began in 1998 when attorney John J. Cummings III purchased Whitney from Formosa Plastics, saving it from demolition. Careful excavations yielded thousands of artifacts, such as gold coins from the 1700s, and unearthed foundations for the first indigo house and first residence, built in the 18th century. In the existing big house, Italian and French artisans have expertly restored Whitney's matchless murals and painted finishes, and no effort or expense was spared to reclaim historic dependencies like the detached kitchen and French barn.

But the major focus of Whitney shifts attention from the plantation big house, however grand, to the slaves upon whom the antebellum culture depended. Cummings intends this to serve as a national slave memorial, has launched massive studies of slave ship manifestos and other obscure records to compile an enormous database, and hopes to interpret the story of slavery in a unique manner, through the children. His Field of Angels, its antique cast-iron fencing featuring little lambs beneath weeping willows, mourns and memorializes the thousands born into slavery on the plantations who died in infancy.

It is believed that Whitney was first established by German immigrant Ambrose Haydel in the early 1700s; his son Jean Jacques probably built the main house around 1790; and the home was formalized with the famous paintings during the occupancy of Ambrose's grandson Marcellin in the 1830s. The Whitney Plantation complex is listed on the National Register of Historic Places as a Historic District.

Though private, the home is under new ownership and there are plans to open the home for tours and other events.

5099 La. Hwy. 18 (River Rd.), Wallace.

Evergreen Plantation
(OPEN FOR TOURS)

In the 1830s this graceful two-story brick structure was most likely adapted from an earlier 1790s Creole home into the Greek Revival style by Ralph Brou. Massive stucco and brick columns support wide galleries and the hip roof, which is topped by a balustrade. Unusual curving double exterior stairs mount to the portico of the second floor, and inside, beautiful period furnishings complement the elegance of the home's design.

But the emphasis here is on a scholarly approach to understanding antebellum plantation culture as a whole. Evergreen is one of the finest examples of a Louisiana planter's house of more than a century ago, and as such the plans and dimensions of the home are now in the National Archives at Washington. However, the real significance of Evergreen must be the huge number of original dependencies surrounding the main house: matching pigeonniers, garçonnieres, stables, detached kitchen, overseer's house, dairy, carriage house, and guesthouse. Even necessities like the lovely little Greek Revival privy had no detail spared in its design.

The tour here provides an unparalleled picture of plantation life as it really was, not only before the Civil War, but afterward, with all the ensuing changes in labor force and finances. Visitors can stroll along the magnificent avenue of live oaks, several centuries old, 39 on each side, that

Evergreen Plantation

extends from the river to the slave quarters along the double row of 22 original cabins. Even sugarcane is still grown on the surrounding acreage.

Evergreen Plantation with its 37 historic structures is a National Historic Landmark and is listed on the National Register of Historic Places. Tours by appointment only. Call (504) 201-3180. Online www.evergreenplantation.org. 4677 La. Hwy. 18 (River Rd.), Edgard.

Glendale Plantation

Built in the opening years of the 19th century, this house is a two-story, cement-covered brick structure with a front gallery a hundred feet wide supported by square wooden pillars. The timbers were hand-hewn and fastened with wooden pegs; the hardware and elaborate mantels were handmade on the place.

Private.

La. Hwy. 18 (River Rd.), below Edgard.

Keller Homestead

Built for Louis Edmond Fortier on a Spanish land grant prior to 1801, this structure has typical French-Spanish architectural design and features a one-inch-thick white plaster veneer on its walls. The house has a fully usable brick-floored basement.

It was later purchased by the Keller family, after whom it was renamed, and was known as Home Place during the Kellers' occupancy.

Keller Homestead is listed on the National Register of Historic Places.

Private.

La. Hwy. 18 (River Rd.), just above Hahnville.

Magnolia Lane

Edgar Fortier built Magnolia Lane in 1784 on 80 arpents of land he received in a Spanish grant. Of West Indian design, this home was located on the original Old Spanish Trail, at that time the only wagon road from the west into New Orleans.

The plantation is historically noted as the land on which Francis Quinette, of St. Louis, grew the first strawberries in Louisiana, and in recent years it has been operated as Nine Mile Point Nursery.

Located across the levee from the house, 600 yards to the north, is the site of Fort Banks. Magnolia Lane is listed on the National Register of Historic Places.
Private.
2141 La. Hwy. 18 (River Rd.), at Nine Mile Point, above Westwego, one mile north of the Huey P. Long Bridge.

Derbigny

This lovely old home, a Louisiana raised cottage typical of the period, was built by Charles Derbigny in the 1830s and named for his father, Pierre, fifth governor of Louisiana, who helped compose Louisiana's civil code. It was originally a 1,500-acre sugarcane plantation.
Private.
La. Hwy. 18 (River Rd.), near Oak Avenue above Westwego.

Tchoupitoulas Plantation

This 19th-century plantation home, built in 1812, housed a popular restaurant for many years but has now returned to use as a residence.
Private.
6535 La. Hwy. 18 (River Rd.), Waggaman.

New Orleans to Donaldsonville
(East Bank, Bayou Lafourche)

Rosella

Built in 1814 by Jean Baptiste Thibodaux, this two-story plantation home has a gallery supported by five brick and plaster columns topped by five slender wooden colonnettes.
Private.
La. Hwy. 308 (east bank of Bayou Lafourche), above Raceland.

Acadia Plantation

The plantation site was said to have been established in the early 19th century by Jim, Rezin, and Stephen Bowie on advice of Jean Lafitte. The present Acadia house, a rambling one-story wooden cottage with ornate gables and dormers, was consolidated from several Creole structures and originally called "Acadie." Subsequent owners through the 19th century included Phillip Key, a relative of Francis Scott Key, composer of "The Star Spangled Banner," and a nephew of Andrew Jackson.

During the Civil War, Acadia was the site of Federal troop encampments.
Private.
La. Hwy. 1 (west bank of Bayou Lafourche), two miles south of Thibodaux.

Chatchie

Boasting weatherboards of hand-shaped cypress, Chatchie is a two-story cottage of early Louisiana colonial construction. Furnishings include an 18th-century piano made in Philadelphia by C. F. L. Albrecht, one of the first made in America.
Private.
La. Hwy. 308 (east bank of Bayou Lafourche), four miles south of Thibodaux.

Rienzi

Of an old-world design, Spanish-style Rienzi boasts twin stairways curving gracefully upward toward the raised entrance. It has a paved lower floor that was originally open to shelter carriages and a gallery that encircles the house. It was constructed in cruciform shape of cypress, cedar, and brick and was named after Cola di Rienzi, 14th-century Italian patriot.

Rienzi was built in 1796, reportedly as a retreat for Queen Maria Louisa of Spain in event of defeat in the Napoleonic Wars. While she never actually occupied the home, her representative, Juan Ygnacia de Egana, purchased the property following the sale of Louisiana to the United States, planted sugarcane, and held great balls and banquets honoring delegates from the Spanish crown.

Later owned by Henry Schuyler Thibodaux, founder of the town of Thibodaux, the house was in the Levert family from 1896 until they generously donated it to the Chef John Folse Culinary Institute at nearby Nicholls State University.

Rienzi is listed on the National Register of Historic Places.

Private.

La. Hwy. 308 (east bank of Bayou Lafourche), Thibodaux.

Rienzi

Laurel Valley Plantation

Laurel Valley Plantation

A huge sugar plantation complex along Bayou Lafourche, Laurel Valley has more than 60 original dependencies remaining on what was a Spanish land grant to Acadian exile Etienne Boudreaux in the 1770s. At the peak of its productive years, more than 350 workers lived here to work the cane crop and man the sugar mill. The surrounding acreage is still in sugar production, and the nonprofit Friends of Laurel Valley operate an interesting little museum store here Wednesdays through Sundays. Call (985) 537-5800. La. Hwy. 308 (east bank of Bayou Lafourche), 2 miles south of Thibodaux.

Madewood Plantation
(OPEN TO PUBLIC)

One of the best-preserved plantation homes of the antebellum period is Madewood, whose name derives from its cypress timbers hand-hewn from trees on the 3,000-acre plantation. Designed by noted architect Henry Howard, the house is considered one of the South's finest examples of pure Greek Revival architecture. It boasts 24-foot ceilings, broad hallways, a magnificent 48-foot-wide ballroom, winding walnut staircase, and more than 20 rooms.

Six Ionic columns, resting on the stylobate rather than on individual pedestals, support the great roof with its peaked pediment. On either side of the main structure are connecting wings echoing its architecture. The interior is dominated by a massive entrance hallway punctuated by Corinthian columns.

Built between 1840 and 1848, Madewood was home to the family of Col. Thomas Pugh of North Carolina, who cultivated 10,000 acres of sugarcane and had 15 children before he died of yellow fever prior to the completion of the house. His widow saved Madewood during the Civil War when its lawns were used as a hospital, and in the 20th century it was reclaimed by the Marshall family after decades of disrepair, a period during which hay was stored in the beautiful ballroom.

Additional historic structures have been moved to the grounds, joining the original detached kitchen and carriage house to form a complex of important buildings from the bayou area.

Madewood Plantation is a National Historic Landmark.

Open daily 10-4; closed major holidays. Entrance fee. Overnight accommodations, weddings, and special events. Call (985) 369-7151. Online www.madewood.com.

4250 La. Hwy. 308 (east bank of Bayou Lafourche), Napoleonville.

Madewood Plantation

Belle Alliance Plantation

Belle Alliance Plantation

This stately 33-room home has wide stairs that ascend above a raised basement to the second floor and lacy iron grillwork on the balcony. It differs from neighboring mansions in its combination of 1830s Classic Revival with the airiness of French Quarter structures. Built in 1847 by Belgian aristocrat Charles Kock, it remained in his family until 1915, its 7,000 acres planted mostly in sugarcane and its sugar house, now crumbling piles of brick, one of the most important west of the Mississippi.

The early settlement here was known as Valenzuela Dans La Fourche, serving as a Spanish military outpost. Today thousands of productive acres planted in sugarcane surround Belle Alliance along Bayou Lafourche.

Private.

La. Hwy. 308 (east bank of Bayou Lafourche), five miles south of Donaldsonville.

St. Emma

St. Emma was built in 1847 by Charles Kock of Belle Alliance, with six square brick and plaster columns supporting the upper gallery and wooden colonnettes supporting the hipped roof.

Private.

La. Hwy. 1 (west bank of Bayou Lafourche), south of Donaldsonville.

Donaldsonville to Houma (West Bank, Bayou Lafourche and Bayou Terrebonne)

Edward Douglass White Historic Site
(OPEN TO PUBLIC)

This home is a simple raised Creole cottage typical of Louisiana 18th-century plantation architecture. It was made of hand-hewn cypress timbers joined with wooden pegs and elevated on tall brick pillars above its basement.

The house was built about 1790 by Edward Douglas White, Sr., judge of the Lafourche Interior Territory, seventh governor of Louisiana from 1835 to 1839, and a member of the U.S. Senate. The home was the birthplace of his son, Edward Douglass White, Jr. (who added another s to his name), Louisiana's most famous jurist. He served on the Louisiana Supreme Court, as a member of the U.S. Senate, and as a justice of the U.S. Supreme Court for nearly three decades, 11 of those years as chief justice.

E. D. White House

The house, with exhibits on bayou culture, is now part of the Louisiana State Museum system, is on the National Register of Historic Places, and has been designated a National Historic Landmark. Open Tuesday-Saturday 8:30-5; closed holidays. Tours and educational living-history events. Entrance fee. Call (985) 447-0915. Online http://lsm.crt.state.la.us/ed_white.htm. 2295 La. Hwy. 1, five miles north of Thibodaux.

Armitage

Built in 1852, Armitage is a fine example of plantation home restoration. This small, beautifully proportioned house was built by Francis L. Mead of Connecticut, who sold the property to Charles Armitage in 1859. It was acquired in 1948 by Mr. and Mrs. Frank Wurzlow, who restored the house and grounds. The front facade remains essentially as it was built, with the addition of three dormers for extra light. One unusual feature is the size of the closets, one 50 feet long and another 18 feet.
Private.
La. Hwy. 20, three miles south of Thibodaux.

Ducros Plantation

Built before the Civil War on land granted by Spain to Thomas Villanueva Barroso, Ducros reportedly was modeled after the Hermitage, Andrew Jackson's Nashville home. A two-story wooden house, it has eight tall square columns supporting wide galleries. A wing was later added to the house on both sides.
The house and plantation were purchased in 1845 or 1846 by Van Perkins Winder, who developed the land into one of the first great sugarcane plantations in Terrebonne Parish. Confederate and Union soldiers occupied the house during the Civil War.
Private.
La. Hwy. 24, half mile north of Schriever.

Sonnier

This plantation home was built in the early 1800s by John G. Potts and is an example of early Louisiana colonial construction. The two-story structure is surrounded by oak, orange, cedar, and magnolia trees.
Private.
La. Hwy. 24, three miles south of Schriever.

Magnolia Plantation

Magnolia Plantation

Constructed in 1834 along Little Bayou Black, this two-story house was built by Thomas Ellis with pleasing simplicity, its double galleries with iron balustrades supported by squared columns without undue embellishment. Ellis's daughter married Confederate general Braxton Bragg here.

Long a productive sugar plantation, during the Civil War, Magnolia was used as a hospital by Federal troops. John Jackson Shaffer bought the property in 1874 and it is still occupied by direct descendents.

Private.

La. Hwy. 311, three miles south of Schriever.

Ardoyne Plantation

Ardoyne Plantation

Ardoyne, its Scottish name meaning "little knoll," is a fairytale castle built by an indulgent husband for a wife who requested a cottage be built for her while she traveled abroad for her health. The "little cottage" to which she returned has a soaring 75-foot tower, bays, arches, and copious Victorian gingerbread copied from a magazine picture of a castle in Scotland.

The home was built in 1897 by the plantation's carpenters and laborers during breaks from the sugarcane harvest. It remains in the family of builder John D. Shaffer and is filled with family treasures. The 60-foot entrance hall, from which rises an immense carved staircase, has a magnificent ceiling of inlaid wood.

Ardoyne is listed on the National Register of Historic Place.

Private.

La. Hwy. 311, seven miles north of Houma.

Ellendale

The land on which Ellendale rests was acquired by Andrew McCollam in 1851. Named for his wife, Ellen, the house contains many treasured family heirlooms. Since its original construction, the house has been enlarged several times. On the grounds still stands one wall of an old sugar mill, a reminder of activities of bygone days.
Private.
La. Hwy. 311, seven miles north of Houma.

Crescent Plantation

William A. Shaffer established this plantation in 1827. The raised cottage, which dates from 1849, is a typical structure of the period with square wooden columns, wide gallery, shutters, and dormer windows. For some time it has housed an attorney's office.
Private.
La. Hwy. 311, three and a half miles north of Houma.

Southdown Plantation House/Terrebonne Museum
(OPEN TO PUBLIC)

It was called "the house that sugar built," and indeed it had more than 10,000 acres of productive cane fields, its own sugar mill, and even its own racetrack. The land here began as a Spanish grant owned in the 1790s by Bowie brothers Jim and Rezin and was purchased by William J. Minor of Natchez in 1828.

Construction of the massive Queen Anne-style house overlooking Little Bayou Black was begun in 1858, its walls of slave-made brick nearly two feet thick in places. The second story was added by Minor's son Henry in 1893. The home has 20 rooms with 14-foot ceilings and is flanked by two turrets. Stained-glass scenes of sugarcane and magnolia blossoms grace the entrance doors.

Minor descendents lost the property during the Depression, and it went through several decades of corporate ownership until a subsidiary of Southdown Sugar donated the house, rear servant's quarters, and surrounding acreage to the Terrebonne Historical and Cultural Society.

Southdown has been beautifully restored and now houses museum exhibits of the sugarcane industry and local culture, a collection of

Southdown Plantation House

porcelain birds, hometown U.S. senator Allen Ellender's memorabilia, and original furniture from the Minor family.

Southdown is listed on the National Register of Historic Places.

Open Tuesday-Saturday, 10-4; last tour begins at 3; closed major holidays. Entrance fee. Call (985) 851-0154. Online www.southdownmuseum.org.

1209 Museum Dr., just off La. Hwy. 311 at St. Charles St., Houma.

Orange Grove

Built between 1846 and 1848, Orange Grove is an outstanding example of the solid building construction of the period. It has been restored to its original beauty, painstakingly preserving the briquette-entre-poteaux (brick between posts) construction and faux bois (false wood grain) treatment of the doors.

Orange Grove is listed on the National Register of Historic Places.

Private.

U.S. Hwy. 90, 12 miles west of Houma.

TOUR 7

Houma to Opelousas
(along Bayou Teche)

Joshua B. Gary House

This beautiful antebellum Greek Revival mansion, which dates from 1839, was built by Joshua B. Gary for his bride, Eleanor Gordy. The entire exterior is cypress, and the interior was constructed with pegs, notches, and square nails.
Private.
9107 La. Hwy. 182, Centerville.

Bocage-on-the-Teche

Once called Oak Bluff Plantation, this 100+-ton house was transported seven miles by barge to its present site on Bayou Teche, surely one of the largest structures ever transferred in this manner. Fairfax Foster Bailey, savior of many historic structures in the Franklin area, relocated, restored, and renamed the one-and-a-half-story home after the sugarcane plantation on which it originally stood became the property of Mrs. Bailey's family.

The Greek Revival structure, built sometime after 1846, stands in a beautiful setting of oaks on Bayou Teche and is an outstanding example of Louisiana antebellum architecture. Theodore Roosevelt was said to have been a guest here more than once.
Private.
9600 La. Hwy. 182, five miles east of Franklin.

Frances

This raised cottage was built around 1810 and is one of the oldest homes along Bayou Teche. The land on which the house stands was granted by Spain to Marc Navarro and was later purchased by Louis

George Demaret. The house remained in the Demaret family until 1879. It was later restored by Fairfax Foster Bailey, whose immediate family produced two state governors from Franklin and who would reclaim many of the area's historic structures.
Private.
10234 La. Hwy. 182, four miles east of Franklin.

Dixie

Constructed of cypress both inside and out, Dixie was built around 1835 by Hilarie Carlin and purchased by Richard A. Wilkins in 1846. Wilkins' sister Sally married Confederate general George Edward Pickett here in 1851.

The house is a two-story structure with a hip roof and four square columns supporting a pedimented portico. It was purchased in 1883 by the first Murphy J. Foster to be Louisiana governor, later a U.S. senator, and was long the home of his granddaughter, Mrs. Langfitt Bowditch Wilby.
Private.
11076 La. Hwy. 182, one and a half miles east of Franklin.

Arlington

This beautiful plantation home was built about 1830 by Euphroisie Carlin, a wealthy planter, on a large land grant. The home's front pedimented portico has four fluted Corinthian columns of wood, which are duplicated in the rear and repeated in modified form on the side porches. The upper and lower balconies are decorated with wrought-iron balustrades.

Arlington is listed on the National Register of Historic Places.
Private.
11532 La. Hwy. 182, on the eastern outskirts of Franklin.

Grevemberg House

Grevemberg House
(OPEN TO PUBLIC)

Built in 1851 by attorney Henry C. Wilson, this stately two-story frame house has four slender Corinthian columns and an upper balcony edged with a balustrade of delicate wooden spindles.

It was acquired in 1857 by the widow of Gabriel Grevemberg after her husband's death in the tragic hurricane that wiped out the popular Victorian seaside resort on Isle Dernier the previous year.

Restored by the St. Mary chapter of the Louisiana Landmarks Society, it houses the St. Mary Parish Museum and is filled with fine period furnishings and interesting exhibits, including an early cast-iron Grevemberg coffin.

Grevemberg House is listed on the National Register of Historic Places.

Open daily 10-4; closed holidays. Call (337) 828-2092. Online www.grevemberghouse.com.

407 Sterling Road (La. Hwy. 322), Franklin.

Oaklawn Manor
(OPEN TO PUBLIC)

This Greek Revival house was built in 1837 by Judge Alexander Porter, an Irishman who became a prominent Louisiana jurist. First a member of the commission that drew up the new state's constitution, he went on to be an associate justice on the first Louisiana Supreme Court, a U.S. senator, and a founder of the Whig Party in Louisiana.

After some lean years following the Civil War, the house was saved by Capt. Clyde A. Barbour, a steamboat captain who had often admired it as he passed along the Teche. He effected many improvements, filled the home with fine period antiques, and planted many of the live oaks that make the setting one of the most beautiful along the bayou.

The George B. Thomsons in the 1960s completely renovated the house, once more resplendent with its 15-foot ceilings, brick walls 20 inches thick, and marble floors. In 1985 it became the much-loved home of former Louisiana governor Murphy J. "Mike" Foster, Jr., and his wife, Alice. Mike Foster is the grandson of the first Governor Foster, who led the state from 1892 to 1900 and then served as U.S. senator until 1913.

Oaklawn Manor is listed on the National Register of Historic Places.

Open Monday-Saturday 10-4; closed Sundays and major holidays. Entrance fee. Call (337) 828-0434. Online www.oaklawnmanor.com.

3296 E. Oaklawn Dr., facing Bayou Teche along Irish Bend Road, five miles northwest of Franklin.

Oaklawn Manor

Darby House

Darby House

One of the finest examples of French colonial architecture in the state and surely one of the oldest structures among the many fine antebellum homes in St. Mary Parish, Darby dates from the eighteenth century's closing years. Perfectly proportioned though small in scale, Darby was built by François St. Mar Darby to please his French wife.

During the Civil War, Union troops rode horses through the house, smashing the fine furnishings. After the war, Darby descendents lived in poverty in the deteriorating home, peddling milk and vegetables to the neighbors.

With exterior stairs connecting double galleries, the home's living quarters were on the top floor above a raised basement. Renovated and operated as a branch bank for some years, Darby is now private.

Private

606 Main St., Baldwin.

Heaton

Built by Albert Heaton in 1853 on a site bordering the Franklin cemetery, this small Italianate villa was moved by barge some 15 miles up Bayou Teche to Linwood, near Charenton, in 1966. Designed by Alexander Jackson Davis, an important architect whose 19th-century house plans appeared in a popular book called *The Architecture of Country Houses,* Heaton is of board and batten construction, its center section rising to a second floor.

Heaton is listed on the National Register of Historic Places.

Private.

2194 Chitimacha Tr., between Baldwin and Charenton.

Alice-Fuselier Home

This early French colonial home, similar in style to Darby, was built by Agricole Fuselier, Sr., at Baldwin around 1800, then moved by barge to its present location and restored by J. Randolph Roane, a descendent of the original builder.

This home is listed on the National Register of Historic Places.

Private.

9217 Old Jeanerette Rd., near Jeanerette.

Alice-Fuselier Home

Albania Plantation

Albania Plantation

Set in a lovely grove of live oaks, this large, stately home has six square wooden columns across the south side and three dormer windows along its gabled roof. This was the carriage entrance to the home in 1842. The actual front of the house faces Bayou Teche to the north, as most early visitors arrived by boat.

Construction of Albania began in 1837 and was completed in 1842. Cypress from the plantation was used to build the house, and red clay from the bayou banks formed the bricks for the foundation. Slave labor built the home, except for the splendid three-story spiral staircase, which was imported from France.

Charles Grevemberg, whose in-laws were the Agricole Fuselier family of nearby Alice-Fuselier Plantation, built Albania. The plantation was expanded by his son to include thousands of acres planted in sugarcane, indigo, corn, and cotton, with its own sugar mill. At one point it was owned by the City of New Orleans, thanks to the will of Isaac Delgado in 1909; its present owner is a widely recognized artist who divides his time between New York and Louisiana.

Albania is listed on the National Register of Historic Places.

Private.

La. Hwy. 182, quarter mile east of Jeanerette.

Enterprise Plantation

Enterprise was built in the 1830s by Simeon Patout of Usay, France, whose original intent, descending as he did from a family of vintners, was to establish a winery here. When he found the soil and hot, humid climate less than ideal for the cultivation of wine grapes, he branched into sugarcane planting with remarkable success.

Patout died in the yellow fever epidemic of 1847, but his family retained ownership of Enterprise, each generation expanding its operations and persisting through hardships like hurricanes, late freezes, financial difficulties, disastrous sugar house fires, and marauding Union soldiers.

Just prior to the Civil War, the plantation mill was making a record 502 hogsheads of sugar annually. Production in the years immediately following the war would be drastically reduced, but by the close of the 20th century M.A. Patout had rebounded and modernized its equipment to become the largest producer of raw sugar in the state, processing more than 12 million tons of sugarcane to produce more than 257 million pounds of sugar.

Today the M.A. Patout & Son, Ltd. corporate headquarters remains here, with members of the Patout family living in the Enterprise house. Listed on the National Register of Historic Places, this is one of the oldest continuously operating sugar plantations and mills still owned and run by descendents of the original family.

Private.

La. Hwy. 85, behind the Sugar House, at Patoutville.

Bayside

Bayside is a two-story double-galleried brick building in the Greek Revival style, with six plastered-brick Doric columns and decorative wooden balustrades. It is surrounded by a magnificent grove of live oaks.

Bayside was built in 1850 by Francis DuBose Richardson, a sugar planter, newspaper correspondent, and philanthropist who served as a member of the Louisiana legislature prior to the Civil War and was a classmate and friend of Edgar Allan Poe.

On the National Register of Historic Places, it is sometimes called the Old Sanders Place because of a later owner.

Private.

La. Hwy. 87, one mile west of Jeanerette.

Joseph Jefferson Home

Joseph Jefferson Home
(OPEN TO PUBLIC)

Built in 1870 by Joseph Jefferson, the world-famous 19th-century actor, this unique structure is made of native cypress cut on Jefferson Island. The original design reflects the influence of Jefferson's travels, combining Moorish, French, and Steamboat Gothic influences, with a rooftop belvedere.

Jefferson won worldwide acclaim for his portrayal of the title role in Washington Irving's "Rip Van Winkle." Pres. Grover Cleveland was among the celebrities who visited Jefferson here.

The house is beautifully complemented by the surrounding Rip Van Winkle Gardens. Begun by J. L. Bayless, Jr., following World War II, the 25-acre, immaculately maintained gardens today offer an enchanting experience throughout every season, with giant gingers, groves of camellias, and azaleas beneath the towering live oaks. The entrance drive is bordered by swampy nesting areas for hundreds of egrets and roseate spoonbills.

Portions of the property were lost in 1980, when a rig drilling exploratory oil wells on Lake Peigneur punctured an underwater salt mine and the entire huge lake and some surrounding land and structures were swallowed up in a giant whirlpool. The Jefferson House, atop its 75-foot elevation, was spared.

The Joseph Jefferson Home is listed on the National Register of Historic Places. Open daily 9-5; last tour at 4. Entrance fee. Overnight accommodations, conference center, and restaurant. Call (337) 359-8525. Online www.ripvanwinklegardens.com. 5505 Rip Van Winkle Rd. off La. Hwy. 675, on Jefferson Island, seven miles southwest of New Iberia.

The Shadows-on-the-Teche
(OPEN TO PUBLIC)

The Shadows-on-the-Teche is one of the fabled antebellum houses of the Deep South. It was built between 1831 and 1834 for wealthy planter David Weeks on the banks of Bayou Teche.

Weeks died in 1834 before his new home was completed, leaving his expectant widow Mary Clara and six small children to move into the Shadows alone. Undaunted, Mary Clara, who eventually remarried Judge John Moore, successfully managed the vast sugar plantation until her death during the Civil War. At that time, the lower floor of the house and outbuildings were occupied by Federal troops and the cemetery was in such disarray that she had to be buried in her own garden.

The late Weeks Hall, descendent of the builder and a noted Louisiana artist, began restoration of the house in 1922. During his period of residence at the Shadows, Weeks Hall entertained numerous celebrities, from Walt Disney to Cecil B. DeMille and Emily Post, all attracted by his exceptional charm and the mysterious appeal of his magnificent home.

In 1958, he bequeathed this notable landmark to the National Trust for Historic Preservation so that the property might be properly interpreted and restored to its appearance during the thirty-year period of residence of his great-grandmother, Mary Clara Conrad Weeks.

The personalities, interests, triumphs, and tragedies of the generations of the Weeks family are very much a part of the interpretation of the Shadows, which has been furnished to realistically reflect their lifestyle. The house contains collections of fine furnishings, family portraits, libraries, silver, and other treasures accumulated over four generations. The Shadows is one of the best-documented house museums in the country, with more than 17,000 family papers and records, and it has been named a National Historic Landmark by the Department of the Interior.

The Shadows-on-the-Teche

The architecture of the beautifully preserved two-story brick house reflects the prevailing classical taste, with eight enormous Tuscan columns across the front and adaptations for the semitropical climate, like the exterior stairs, wide galleries, upstairs living quarters, and plenty of cross-ventilation. It is situated among lofty live oaks providing cooling shade, and the lush tropical plantings surrounding the house contribute to its unique charm.

Open daily 9-4:30, Sundays from noon; closed major holidays. Entrance fee. Call (337) 369-6446. Online www.shadowsontheteche.org. 317 E. Main Street (La. Hwy. 182), New Iberia.

Mintmere

Built during the decade before the Civil War, Mintmere is a handsome Greek Revival raised cottage enhanced by a lawn stretching to Bayou Teche. The house has been restored and is listed on the National Register of Historic Places.
Private.
1400 E. Main St. (La. Hwy. 182), New Iberia.

Holleman House

The original house on this site was known as Segura House, constructed about 1812. Extended abandonment and two hurricanes damaged the house extensively, so a Segura descendent dismantled and rebuilt the house using materials and dimensions from the original.
Private.
La. Hwy. 182, west of New Iberia.

Dulcito Plantation

Set in a grove of trees on the banks of Spanish Lake (Lake Tasse), Dulcito was built around 1788 by Dauterive Dubuclet as a summer home. During the Civil War it was used as a Confederate field hospital.

Its architectural style is typical of early Louisiana homes: raised on high pillars, with long gables and wide rambling galleries. The heavy cypress timbers of the frame and the exposed beams are fastened with wooden pegs. Traces of the structure's original adobe walls may still be seen.

Later purchased by the Trappey family, Dulcito has been beautifully restored and is listed on the National Register of Historic Places.
Private.
La. Hwy. 182, seven miles west of New Iberia.

St. John

This large frame house set in a grove of trees has four tall wooden columns of classic style, a hipped roof, and a belvedere. It was built in 1828 by Alexandre Etienne de Clouet, descendent of the Chevalier Alexandre de Clouet, early commandant of the Poste des Attakapas. A large wooded tract near the plantation was maintained as a deer park by de Clouet.
Private.
La. 347, three miles north of St. Martinville.

Maison Olivier

Maison Olivier/
Longfellow-Evangeline State Historic Site
(OPEN TO PUBLIC)

This property was purchased by the state in 1931 and opened as the first state park. Through its components it relates the story of early Acadian settlement patterns and daily life on a vacherie, or cattle ranch, here in what was the Attakapas District among the open prairie ranges that furnished beef for New Orleans markets.

Maison Olivier is a classic raised Creole cottage built circa 1815 on a royal French land grant by Pierre Olivier Duclozel de Vezin, its lower floor of Bayou Teche clay brick, its upper floor of bousillage insulation between cypress uprights, its kitchen detached from the main building. Also on park grounds is the rustic Acadian Farmstead, the steep-roofed cabin furnished simply, with outdoor bread oven, barn, and small herd of longhorn cattle.

Maison Olivier is a National Historic Landmark, and the venerable Gabriel Oak that shades it recalls Evangeline's lost lover in Longfellow's epic poem of the Acadian exiles.

Open daily 9-5; closed holidays. Entrance fee. Interpretive programs. Call (337) 394-3754. Online www.crt.state.la.us/parks.

120 N. Main Street, north of St. Martinville.

Huron

This well-preserved plantation home was built before 1850 by Charles Lastrapes, member of one of the old Creole families of the Attakapas country.
Private.
La. Hwy. 347, four and a half miles south of Arnaudville.

Robin

Robin is a one-and-a-half-story cottage built around 1830 by Numa Robin, grandson of Napoleon Robin, a French general who immigrated to America after Bonaparte was exiled.
Private.
La. Hwy. 31 at Bayou Teche, below Leonville.

TOUR 8
Natchitoches to Opelousas

Wells Home
One of the oldest homes in Louisiana, and said to be one of the oldest still standing in the Mississippi River valley, this is the most authentically restored antebellum residence in Natchitoches. It was constructed about 1776 by Gabriel Buard and features hand-hewn cypress sills and rafters joined with wooden pegs. The walls are adobe mixed with dried moss and deer hair. Once known as the Williams-Tauzin home, this structure was originally used as a way station for goods being shipped west of the river.
Private.
607 Williams Ave., Natchitoches.

Lemee House
(OPEN BY APPOINTMENT)
Constructed by an Italian contractor named Soldini in the 1830s, this European-style structure serves as the headquarters for the Association for the Preservation of Historic Natchitoches. One of the few houses of the period with a cellar for smoked meats and wines, this one-and-a-half-story plastered brick home featuring a cradle roof is a Natchitoches landmark.
The Lemee House serves as headquarters for the annual Fall Tour, sponsored by the Association for the Preservation of Historic Natchitoches, during the second weekend in October. Call (318) 357-7907 for appointments for group tours.
310 Jefferson St., Natchitoches.

Roque House
Constructed without nails in the early 1800s by a freedman of color named Yves, the Roque House is an excellent example of early Creole construction. It is built with cypress beams and bousillage, walls filled with mud, animal hair, and moss. It is named after its last occupant,

Madame Aubin Roque, granddaughter of Augustin Metoyer, wealthy Creole landowner of Isle Brevelle, south of the city, in antebellum days. In 1967, Museum Contents, Inc., a nonprofit organization, acquired the house and moved it to the present location on the riverbank below Front Street. The structure is topped with an oversized roof of durable cypress shingles, forming a gallery around the house's exterior. Restoration was undertaken by the same organization. Its most recent occupants have been commercial.
Private.
Riverfront Dr., Natchitoches.

Prud'homme-Rouquier House

An excellent example of French vernacular half-timbered architecture and considered one of the largest examples of bousillage construction in the country, the home was originally part of a working cotton plantation. It was built by Frances Rouquier, whose father was stationed at the 18th-century Fort St. Jean Baptiste and who in 1782 married Marie Louise Prud'homme. The original French Creole architecture was modernized around 1825 by Rouquier's daughter and her husband, with the resultant facade showing Federal and Greek Revival influences. The nonprofit Service League of Natchitoches owns the house today.
Private.
Jefferson St., Natchitoches.

Tante Huppé House

(OPEN TO PUBLIC)
In the heart of Natchitoches's National Landmark Historic District, this home has played an important part in the lives of generations of area residents. The two-story structure was built for Suzette Prudhomme, Tante Huppé, around 1830. She was thrice married and her only son died in 1835. Until her death in 1861, Prudhomme lived alone, but her home hosted many relatives visiting in Natchitoches from neighboring plantations.
The house contains 18 rooms. Walls are of cypress with brick between, typical of early Louisiana construction, and there are slave quarters behind. The house has nine fireplaces and 11 outside doors, and all of the locks, keys, curtain rods, and glass panes are original. The Tante Huppé House was restored in 1968 by a descendent long active in historic preservation statewide.
Tours by appointment. Overnight accommodations. Call (318) 352-5342. Online www.tantehuppe.com.
424 Jefferson St., Natchitoches.

Oaklawn Plantation

One of the distinguishing features of this beautiful antebellum house is the long avenue of live oak trees lining the front drive, at 680 feet one of the longest in Louisiana. Oaklawn was begun around 1830 by Narcisse Prudhomme for his son, Pierre Achille Prudhomme. The architecture is that of the raised Louisiana cottage style typical of the period, brick on the first level and wood on the second floor with adobe walls. The framework is hand-hewn cypress, pegged and mortised. The house remains for the most part in its original form.

Oaklawn is listed on the National Register of Historic Places.
Private.
La. Hwy. 494, seven miles south of Natchitoches.

Cherokee Plantation

Cherokee, built between 1830 and 1840, is named for the Cherokee roses that adorn the front yard. The hip-roofed West Indies-style house is built in raised-cottage fashion atop 36 brick piers, with massive cypress beams and bousillage insulation. The six original fireplaces and tall folding doors of faux bois (false wood) add to the character of the house.

The plantation was first known as the Emile Sompayrac Place. Robert Calvert Murphy purchased Cherokee in 1890, and it was been restored and furnished with fine Murphy family antiques.

Cherokee is listed on the National Register of Historic Places.
Private.
La. Hwy. 494, about seven miles south of Natchitoches.

Beau Fort Plantation

This wide cottage-style home, said to have been built on the site of a 1760s fort, may date back as far as the 1790s, when the land grant property was occupied by Louis Barthelemy Rachel. Narcisse Prudhomme purchased it at auction in 1834, after which he and his son considerably enlarged the plantation.

Not a typical raised Creole cottage and yet showing signs of Creole influence, it was built of cypress and bousillage, with an 84-foot gallery across the front. The current name was given to the home by Mr. and Mrs. C. Vernon Cloutier, who restored the house and grounds in the 1940s.

Beau Fort is listed on the National Register of Historic Places.
Private.
La. Hwy. 494, about 10 miles south of Natchitoches.

Oakland Plantation
(OPEN TO PUBLIC)

Built between 1818 and 1821 by slave labor, the plantation house is a large raised home with a 10-foot-deep veranda on all sides. Only the finest heart-of-cypress woods, joined entirely without nails, were used in its construction. Walls of the supporting foundation are of brick and adobe, held together by deer hair and moss. The builder was Jean Pierre Emmanuel Prudhomme, the third generation of his family in America and a successful planter of cotton, tobacco, and indigo.

A fascinating array of original outbuildings—pigeonniers, overseer's house, log corncrib, carriage house, mule barn, carpenter's shop, chicken coops, and cabins—remain to vividly illustrate antebellum plantation life. The movie *The Horse Soldiers,* with John Wayne, was filmed here.

A classic example of French colonial style, Oakland is listed on the National Register of Historic Places, is a National Bicentennial Farm and a National Historic Landmark, and is also a unit of Cane River Creole National Historical Park.

Open daily 8-4 for self-guided tours through dependencies; guided tour through main house at 1. Call (318) 356-8441. Online www.nps.gov/cari.

4386 La. Hwy. 494, 10 miles south of Natchitoches.

Oakland Plantation

Melrose Plantation
(OPEN TO PUBLIC)

According to tradition, this plantation was originally known as Yucca Plantation when it was established in the late 18th century by the family of the remarkable Marie Therese Coincoin. Born a slave in 1742, she was freed by the French merchant Claude Thomas Pierre Metoyer, with whom she produced 10 children who became the ancestors of the extensive Isle Brevelle community of Creoles of color. As she and her sons planted crops and prospered, they purchased the freedom of her other offspring and obtained a number of land grants, including the Melrose property.

The earliest structure on the place was probably the Yucca House, built of cypress beams chinked with mud and moss. The 1800 African House has been named one of the most distinctive buildings in the south, a square hut with a steep shingled hip roof overhanging far enough to shelter teams and wagons. Louis Metoyer built the main house on the plantation around 1833.

The Hertzog family owned the property and planted crops through the mid-19th century. Through much of the 20th century it was owned by the Henry family, who grew cotton and renamed the place after the Melrose Abbey in Scotland. Melrose became a haven for writers and a center of the arts through the efforts of Mrs. Cammie Garrett Henry. Among the many authors who enjoyed her hospitality over the years were Lyle Saxon, Alexander Woollcott, Gwen Bristow, and Harnett Kane.

Clementine Hunter, called "the black Grandma Moses" for her primitive paintings depicting early Cane River plantation life, was once a field hand and cook here, and her colorful murals still line the upper walls of the African House. When she died at 101, her work was in great demand around the world.

Now owned by the Association for the Preservation of Historic Natchitoches, Melrose is listed on the National Register of Historic Places and has been designated a National Historic Landmark.

Open Tuesday-Sunday noon-4; closed Mondays and holidays. Entrance fee. Call (318) 379-0055. Online www.caneriverheritage.org. 2522 La. Hwy. 494, 16 miles south of Natchitoches.

Melrose Plantation

African House at Melrose

Magnolia Plantation
(OPEN TO PUBLIC)

A two-and-a-half-story house with 27 rooms and a Catholic chapel, the present Magnolia was built on the foundations of a home burned during the Civil War. Still standing at Magnolia are the orderly rows of original brick slave quarters showing an unusual degree of architectural refinement for such structures.

Ambrose Lecompte II, who would become the largest cotton producer in the parish by the time of the Civil War, built the main house around 1840. After the war it was rebuilt by his daughter and son-in-law, Matthew Hertzog.

Surrounding the main house are original dependencies, including blacksmith shop, plantation store, pigeonnier, overseer's Acadian cottage/slave hospital, and gin barn, which houses the country's last wooden screw-type cotton press, dating from 1830, remaining in its original site.

Magnolia is listed on the National Register of Historic Places and is a unit of the Cane River Creole National Historical Park.

The main house is private, but the plantation complex with 18 acres of outbuildings is open daily 8-4; closed major holidays. Entrance fee. Call (318) 356-8441. Online www.nps.gov/cari.

La. Hwy. 119, one mile north of Derry.

Magnolia Plantation quarters housing

Little Eva Plantation

Previously known by various names, including Hidden Hill and Chopin Plantation, this property was renamed for the brave little heroine of Harriet Beecher Stowe's sensational book *Uncle Tom's Cabin*. According to legend, Stowe visited the area in the 1840s and was said to have used one early planter, New Englander Robert McAlpin, as the model for cruel slave owner Simon Legree in her antislavery novel. Stowe herself insisted her characters were fictional composites based on many sources. Despite continual controversy as to whether Little Eva was the book's setting, one of the plantation's cabins was restored and exhibited as the "Original Uncle Tom's Cabin" at the 1893 Chicago World's Fair, and for a time there was even a tour to "Uncle Tom's Grave" on the property.

Today Little Eva is a working pecan plantation with several thousand acres of trees and sales outlets along the highway.

Private.

La. Hwy. 1 at Chopin, four miles south of Cloutierville.

Castille Plantation

Facing Bayou Rapides is Castille, a raised cottage with a gabled roof. It was built prior to 1840 and remains a 3,500-acre cotton plantation.

Private.

Bayou Rapides Rd., seven miles from La. Hwy. 1.

Eden Plantation

Eden was first owned by James Griffin and used as a Methodist school. The one-and-a-half-story frame house was built by Benjamin Kitchen Hunter before the Civil War.

Private.

Bayou Rapides Rd., seven and a half miles from La. Hwy. 1.

Tyrone Plantation

(OPEN BY APPOINTMENT)

Built in 1843 as the center of a 1,200-acre cotton plantation, Tyrone has since been considerably remodeled. Previous owners included General Sprague of New Orleans and Gen. Mason Graham.

Open for group tours by appointment. Overnight accommodations. Call (318) 442-8528.

6576 Bayou Rapides Rd., Alexandria.

Cedar Grove

The original Cedar Grove house may have dated from the mid-1700s, according to papers found in an old chimney in the house. It was remodeled in the 1820s or 1830s and recently completely rebuilt.
Private.
Bayou Rapides Rd., about 15 miles from La. Hwy. 1.

Kent Plantation House
(OPEN TO PUBLIC)

On the National Register of Historic Places, Kent House is believed to be the oldest standing structure in central Louisiana, where many historic homes were burned during the Civil War, and it is a fine example of rural Louisiana plantation architecture. The central section, built between 1796 and 1800 by French settler Pierre Baillio II, is of red-clay mud and moss—"bousillage"—between cypress beams. The flanking wings were added in the 1840s by second owner Robert Hynson. Both portions of the house are raised high above ground on brick piers. Inside are seven period rooms decorated with outstanding examples of Federal, Sheraton, and Empire furniture, as well as pieces made by native Louisiana cabinetmakers.

The fully furnished house and its dependencies—detached kitchen,

Kent Plantation House

milk house, herb garden, barns, and sugar-making apparatus—provide a vivid picture of 19th-century life. Open Monday-Saturday 9-5; closed holidays. Living-history demonstrations; lively fall Sugar Day. Weddings and events. Entrance fee. Call (318) 487-5998. Online www.kenthouse.org. 3601 Bayou Rapides Rd., Alexandria.

New Hope

This well-preserved two-story plantation house was built in 1816 by a member of the Tanner family. Although remodeled, it retains the original frame house and foundation of heavy cypress timbers. It is often referred to as the Gordon Place.

The house has wide porches that run the full length of the upper and lower floors, and slender wooden columns support the hip roof. New Hope faces Bayou Boeuf.

Private.

Off U.S. Hwy. 71, two miles south of Meeker.

Loyd Hall

(OPEN TO PUBLIC)

The uncertain history of this mysterious two-and-a-half-story brick structure enhances interest in it. Recent documentation indicates that the house was built shortly before the Civil War. Its owner wished to build the showplace of the Bayou Boeuf area, but his elderly neighbor, Civil War governor James Madison Wells, called the house "Loyd's Folly."

Loyd Hall features a double porch with white columns and iron lace trim. It faces north, overlooking Bayou Boeuf and near the old Loyd Bridge, which was used by travelers heading west along the Texas Trail.

Legend has it that the house acquired its present spelling when a wayward member of the Lloyd family of England was given the property with the proviso that he leave Europe and change his name.

The house, with rooms 20' by 20' by 16', was restored by Mrs. Virginia Fitzgerald, retaining the original heart-pine flooring, cypress woodwork, and mahogany staircases. New ownership in 2007 meant extensive restoration then as well.

Loyd Hall is listed on the National Register of Historic Places.

Open for group tours by appointment. Special events. Overnight accommodations. Entrance fee. Call (318) 776-5641. Online www.loydhall.com. 292 Loyd Bridge Rd., Cheneyville.

Wytchwood

Built on Bayou Boeuf of hand-hewn cypress timbers held together with wooden pins, Wytchwood stands at the end of a long avenue of moss-draped live oaks.

Wytchwood is owned by the Robert Munson family, whose ancestors, Robert and Providence Tanner, settled the land around 1813.
Private.
Off U.S. Hwy. 71, just south of Loyd Hall, Cheneyville.

Wright Plantation/Oakwold

Surrounded by mammoth oak trees, this two-story structure has a red brick foundation and a porch with Doric columns of wood enclosing three sides. It was built in 1835 by S. M. Perkins, a Wright family ancestor. According to family tradition, Sam Houston was lavishly entertained at this home on two occasions. It is now called Oakwold.
Private.
On La. Hwy. 29.

Homeplace

Known for many years as the Wikoff Place, Homeplace is a one-and-a-half-story structure shaded by a splendid grove of oaks. It was built in 1826 on a Spanish land grant made in 1791 to Dr. François Robin, a native of France and a doctor of medicine and law.
Private.
La. Hwy. 182, Beggs, on Bayou Boeuf north of Washington.

Magnolia Ridge

(GROUNDS OPEN FOR WALKING)
Completed in 1830, this superb mansion is surrounded by 60 acres of landscaped grounds. During the Civil War, it was headquarters for both Confederate and Federal forces.

Built on a knoll overlooking Bayou Courtableau, the two-and-a-half-story brick house has six Doric columns of plaster-covered brick that support the heavy cornice of the gabled roof.

Open daylight hours in good weather for walking; three-mile asphalt walkway through grounds. House is private. Call (337) 8926-3027.
Prescott St., Washington.

Arlington
This brick house was built by Maj. Amos Webb in 1829 and has been completely restored. Among its distinctive features are a wide central hallway of Italian flagstone on the lower level, a similar hallway reached by a mahogany-railed staircase on the second floor, and a large schoolroom on the third story.
Private.
DeJean St. (La. Hwy. 103), two miles from Washington.

Wartelle House
This house is approached through one of the longest and most beautiful avenues of water oaks in Louisiana. Built in 1829 by Pierre Gabriel Wartelle, a captain in Napoleon's army who came to Louisiana after Bonaparte's exile to Elba, this one-story rambling frame structure has a hipped dormer roof.
Private.
West of Washington near Arlington.

Starvation Point
This large, rather elaborate brick plantation home was built around 1790 at the confluence of Bayous Boeuf and Cocodrie. It was originally an inn patronized by boatmen bringing produce and goods to and from Bayou Courtableau. The house was later used by both Union and Confederate officers during the Civil War.
Starvation Point is listed on the National Register of Historic Places.
Private.
La. Hwy. 746, two and a half miles north of Washington.

Means Plantation House
Set in a grove of magnolia and oak trees, this late-18th-century structure was the residence of an early French aristocrat, the Chevalier Florentin Poiret. Round brick pillars of the lower gallery support smaller cypress columns of the upper. The home was restored by the J. C. Means family.
Private.
La. Hwy. 10 near Opelousas.

Estorge House

Estorge House

One of the older homes in the Opelousas area, this Greek Revival residence, featuring trompe l'oeil ceilings in the entrance hall and parlor, was constructed with slave labor about 1827 for Pierre Labyche.

The Estorge House is listed on the National Register of Historic Places and was for a time a bed and breakfast.

Private.

417 North Market St., Opelousas.

Doucet House

A typical 18th-century Louisiana French home, Doucet House features arched cypress transoms over the 10 French doors, which came from the old St. Landry Courthouse.

The lower floor is constructed of brick, while the upper story is made of wood. One-story garçonnieres are joined to each side of the house by covered galleries.

Private.

Near Opelousas.

Michel Prudhomme House

Michel Prudhomme House

Michel Prudhomme was born in Strasbourg, France, in 1739 and came to Louisiana in 1759. He moved to the Poste des Opelousas, became a successful planter, and built this two-story French colonial home in the late 1700s.

The house was sold to the Ringrose family in 1894 and then to the Fontenot family in 1945. It is presently owned by the Preservationists of St. Landry, Inc. Now engulfed by the local hospital complex, it is opened only for meetings and tours by advance arrangement with board members.

1152 Prudhomme Circle, Opelousas.

Linwood

Constructed in 1856 by Michel D. Boatwright and Caleb L. Swayze, Linwood was acquired by Dr. Vincent Boagni in 1867. Legend has it that the ghost of Capt. Jack Thompson, son-in-law of Dr. Boagni, frequently appears on the grounds.

Private.

Near Opelousas.

TOUR 8A
Shreveport to Mansfield

Buena Vista

This home, listed on the National Register of Historic Places, was built by Boykin Witherspoon of South Carolina. It is a three-story wooden house with octagonal wooden columns across the front. The gallery floor is detached from the columns, which are set in square brick bases. Within the home is an interesting square staircase, built when the house was erected between 1854 and 1859. To the rear stand the original cook house and a square, hand-hewn cypress log cabin that predates the home.

Private.

Four miles south of Stonewall on La. Hwy. 171, left on Red Bluff Rd. for one and a half miles.

Roseneath

Built in the 1840s, Roseneath was the plantation home of the Means family—a name long part of the history of this area. The home is a two-story wooden structure with square wooden pillars on the upper and lower galleries, and has a galleried ell to the rear. At each end of the shingled, gabled roof is an outside chimney.

This building is listed on the National Register of Historic Places.

Private.

La. Hwy. 5 between La. Hwy. 171 and 175, near Gloster.

Fairview

This raised cottage was constructed in 1848 on an original Spanish land grant. Complementing the splendid front gallery are French windows. Confederate soldiers camped here en route to the Battle of Mansfield.

There is a family cemetery near the road.

Private.

La. Hwy. 172, about four miles past Keatchie.

93

Caspiana House

Caspiana House
(OPEN TO PUBLIC)

The main house of Caspiana plantation has been moved to serve as the focal point of the Pioneer Heritage Center in Shreveport. The house is of Georgian architecture, built in 1856, and was donated by the heirs of builder William J. Hutchinson. It is listed on the National Register of Historic Places.

The historical complex is composed of six authentic plantation structures of pioneer northwest Louisiana, including the detached kitchen from the Webb plantation, an 1860 double-pen log house, and an early doctor's office, complete with vintage medical instruments. Trained volunteers interpret everyday life in the 19th century, the period of settlement and early development in the Red River region around Shreveport.

On the campus of Louisiana State University in Shreveport. Group tours and school tours by appointment. Call (318) 797-5339.

University Place betweeen La. Hwy. 1 (Youree Dr.) and East Kings Hwy., Shreveport.

TOUR 8B

Lake Charles to Opelousas

Imperial Calcasieu Museum
(OPEN TO PUBLIC)

This colonial-style building was constructed of beams from historic homes in the area, bricks from the Missouri Pacific Railroad Station, and columns from the old Majestic Hotel, which once graced Lake Charles. It is now a museum housing memorabilia from a century or more ago, including a 1607 "Breeches Bible," a ship's wheel, and life-size scenes of 19th-century life, complete with barber shop, apothecary, kitchen, and bedroom. In the rear of the museum is the ancient spreading Sallier Oak, a 300+-year-old tree named for Charles Sallier, for whom Lake Charles was named.

Open Tuesday-Saturday 10-5. Call (337) 439-3797. Online www.imperialcalcasieumuseum.org.

204 West Sallier St., Lake Charles.

LeBleu Plantation House

This one-story home, formerly two stories, has a lower front gallery supported by six square cypress columns and supposedly includes within its walls materials from the first dwelling ever built in this area by white settlers.

Lafitte and his pirate band were said to have held meetings in the plantation's barn, which was destroyed in 1918. A later owner, "Grandma Joe" LeBleu, claimed to have fed two strangers who turned out to be Jesse James and his brother, Frank.

Private.

U.S. Hwy. 90, about five miles west of Iowa.

Estherwood Manor

This stately two-story Greek Revival home has 18 rooms, five bedrooms on the second floor, five marble fireplaces, and large twin parlors that feature Gothic ceilings.

Private.

U.S. Hwy. 90, 10 miles west of Crowley.

Crystal Rice Heritage Farm

(OPEN BY APPOINTMENT)

A working rice farm since Salmon Wright began his quest for new varieties of the grain in 1890, the lands of the Crystal Rice Plantation are still worked by his descendents, who have added crawfish as well.

A cypress Acadian cottage, built in 1848, was moved from Youngsville to become the Blue Rose Museum, full of collections of fine china, cut glass, silver, and antique furniture. Also on display are antique cars in Salmon's Classic Car Garage.

Open for agricultural tours, cooking classes, and museum tours. Call (337) 783-6417. Online www.crystalrice.com.

6428 Airport Rd., five miles southwest of Crowley.

Alexandre Mouton House/Lafayette Museum

(OPEN TO PUBLIC)

The former home of Alexandre Mouton, Louisiana's first Democratic governor, this structure was built in 1800 by his father, Jean Mouton, founder of Vermilionville, as Lafayette was first known. He built this as his Sunday House, a large one-room house with a kitchen added at the back. Governor Mouton added three rooms to it and in 1849, when it was sold to Dr. W. G. Mills, the second and third floors and rooftop lookout tower were added.

The museum displays Carnival costumes, antiques, paintings, and historic newspapers and documents in both French and English.

The Lafayette Museum is listed on the National Register of Historic Places.

Open Tuesday-Saturday 9-5; Sunday 1-4; closed Monday and holidays. Call (337) 234-2208.

1122 Lafayette St., Lafayette.

Shady Oaks

Built in 1848 for Jean Mouton's grandson Charles Homere Mouton, Shady Oaks has a lower floor of handmade brick and an upper floor of cypress. Blending French and Anglo-American design, the house has been restored many times, but it retains its original charm and architectural features. Private.
338 North Sterling St., Lafayette.

Vermilionville

(OPEN TO PUBLIC)

A Cajun-Creole heritage and folklife park, village tells the stories of the French-speaking Acadian exiles as they arrived in Louisiana beginning in the 1750s. There are six restored historic homes, 13 reproduction period buildings, and exhibits of the cultures influencing the Acadian arrivals.

One of the original buildings is Fausse Pointe, home of Amand Broussard, son of the famous Acadian resistance fighter Joseph Beausoleil Broussard, who led 250 Acadians to Louisiana after they were forced from their homes in Acadie, Nova Scotia. Other structures replicate the church, schoolhouse, trapper's cabin, blacksmith shop, barns, and other necessities of pioneer life.

Living-history demonstrations by costumed bilingual staff showcase Cajun and Zydeco music, Cajun cooking, carpentry, spinning, and other crafts.
Open Tuesday-Sunday 10-3; closed holidays. Entrance fee. Restaurant. Special events and weddings. Call (337) 233-4077. Online www.vermilionville.org.
300 Fisher Rd., Lafayette.

Myrtle Plantation House

Built in 1811 by Dr. Matthew Creighton, the first physician to practice in the city of Lafayette, this antebellum home has been added to by each succeeding generation. Creighton is famous for having failed the first medical licensure test ever given in Louisiana. He sued, and in court he was able to recall all the questions of the test and give the answers from memory! In spite of the remarkable feat, he lost his suit, but he passed the next examination.

The present hall of the house, with its hand-hewn stairway at the rear, was originally the front porch and was closed in with shutters and transoms.

On the canvas walls and ceiling of the present dining room are landscape scenes painted in the late 19th century by Charles de Bubuire, a French artist who had worked on the old French Opera House in New Orleans. Private.
Hugh Wallis Rd., near Lafayette.

Chretien Point

Chretien Point

This two-story brick home was built in 1831 by Hypolite Chretien II on land given as a wedding gift from his father, Hypolite I. Originally granted to Pierre Declouet by the Spanish government in 1776, the land came under Chretien ownership at the close of the 18th century. The mansion is built on a slight rise, which adds to its massive stateliness. It has six columns set in square bases rising past the upper gallery to the hip roof. Three large doors, each separated by a window, open onto the first- and second-floor galleries. Both doors and windows have graceful arches at the top.

Lafitte the pirate was said to have been a close friend of the elder Chretien and a frequent visitor to the plantation.

Chretien Point is listed on the National Register of Historic Places. Long a popular bed and breakfast and tour home, it is now private, though plans for tours are in the works.

Private.

665 Chretien Point Rd., Sunset.

TOUR 9
Opelousas to New Roads

Woodley Plantation

This one-and-a-half-story frame house, well over a century old, is located on the plantation established by Isaac Johnson, governor of Louisiana from 1846 to 1850, after he moved to this area from West Feliciana Parish.
Private.
La. Hwy. 411, one mile south of Livonia.

Sunnyside

Built in the mid-1800s on the east bank of Bayou Grosse Tete, Sunnyside is a raised cottage with a cypress upper story over a plastered-brick basement. Its double galleries are supported by square cypress columns and simple balustrades.

First owned by Capt. Jesse Hart, it has been in the possession of members of the Johnson and Woolfolk families as well as heirs of Bartholomew Barrow of the pioneering Barrows who moved from the Carolinas to West Feliciana in the late 1700s and then spread west into Pointe Coupee and Iberville Parishes as the family expanded.
Private.
La. Hwy. 77, near Maringouin.

El Dorado

Once owned by the famous Barrow family of the Felicianas, El Dorado is a beautiful dormered cottage that dates from the early 1800s. The home is listed on the National Register of Historic Places.

Of special interest is the two-story brick slave quarters structure, located directly behind the main house.
Private.
La. Hwy. 77, near Maringouin.

Tanglewild

Built prior to the Civil War by Bartholomew Barrow and now set within a grove of giant live oaks, Tanglewild is a stately one-and-a-half-story frame structure, well restored.
Private.
La. Hwy. 77, directly across from the Bayou Grosse Tete Bridge, near Maringouin.

Mound Plantation

Constructed by Austin Woolfolk in 1840, the main house on Mound Plantation was named after the Indian mound on which it was built. It is a rambling one-and-a-half-story frame cottage, with an ell on one side. In the rear is a slave laundry made of brick.

During the construction, a number of Indian relics were uncovered, including human skeletons.
Private.
La. Hwy. 77, three miles south of Maringouin.

Shady Grove Plantation

One of many plantations once owned by Capt. Joseph Irwin, Shady Grove was purchased from him by his son in 1828. The house, built in 1858, is a two-story brick structure with wooden Ionic columns on the lower floor and Corinthian columns on the upper. The house is used as the North Iberville High School.
Private.
La. Hwy. 77, about four miles south of Maringouin.

Live Oaks Plantation

The plantation was established in the early 1800s by Charles Dickinson of Tennessee, whose grandfather, Capt. Joseph Irwin, became his guardian after Dickinson's father was killed in a duel with Andrew Jackson.

The graceful main house of two and a half stories has galleries across the front supported by six square wooden pillars. Today it sits in a magnificent grove of live oaks, one of which has a circumference of almost 30 feet. Within the grove is a brick slave church.

Live Oaks Plantation is listed on the National Register of Historic Places.
Private.
La. Hwy. 77, just north of Rosedale.

Trinity Plantation

Dr. George Campbell of New Orleans purchased the plantation lands in 1839. The main house was built facing Bayou Grosse Tete. It is a plaster-covered brick structure standing on an Indian mound and is situated at the end of a splendid avenue of live oaks. Of Greek Revival design, it features a gable parapet roof of a type rarely seen in this area. Trinity Plantation is listed on the National Register of Historic Places. Private.

La. Hwy. 77, southern end of Rosedale.

Austerlitz

A classic early two-story frame house with a brick basement, Austerlitz is encircled by a gallery 80 feet wide and 14 feet deep. The house faces False River, once the main channel of the Mississippi.

The second floor is of cypress, reinforced with brick and mortar. It has square wooden pillars below and slender columns above, and both upper and lower entrances are fanlighted.

Austerlitz was built in 1832 on land purchased from two Indian chiefs by Joseph Decuir in 1797. An architect was brought in from Santo Domingo to design the house, which accounts for its decided West Indies influence. In 1899, a two-story annex was added, increasing the number of rooms to 22.

The house, on the National Register of Historic Places, was named for one of Napoleon Bonaparte's battles. Locke Breaux, brother of Chief Justice Joseph Breaux of the Louisiana Supreme Court, was a later owner. Private.

La. Hwy. 1, six miles south of New Roads, along False River.

Parlange Plantation
(OPEN BY APPOINTMENT)

Built in 1750 by the Marquis Vincent de Ternant on a land grant from the French crown, Parlange is one of Louisiana's oldest and most charming plantation homes. It is a superb example of French colonial plantation architecture, designed for comfort and fashioned of materials at hand, and remains one of the least altered examples of the period.

Its two stories are a raised brick basement and a second floor of living space made of cypress, with twin chimneys. Galleries completely encircle the house and remain the favored spot for entertaining guests and enjoying the cooling breezes across the waters of False River, the oxbow lake cut off by the Mississippi.

Matching dovecotes flank the entrance drive. These rare pigeonniers are octagonal, constructed of handmade brick, and beautifully restored.

Originally an indigo plantation, Parlange was switched to sugarcane by de Ternant's son Claude in the 19th century, and he became one of the most successful of Louisiana's sugar planters. Claude's wife, Virginie, during lengthy sojourns in Paris, acquired many of the fine furnishings and superb portraits still in Parlange. Upon the death of de Ternant, she married Col. Charles Parlange, whose name has endured for both family and plantation. Virginie's son Charles Parlange became a respected statesman and judge, while her daughter, Marie Virginie de Ternant Avegno, was the subject of painter John Singer Sargent's masterpiece called *Portrait of Madame X*, now hanging in the Metropolitan Museum of Art in New York.

Occupied by both Gen. Nathaniel Banks of the Union army and Gen. Richard Taylor of the Confederacy at different times during the Red River Campaign of 1864, Parlange remains a working plantation, surrounded by extensive fields of crops and cattle. It has been occupied by the gracious descendents of the original builder since the 18th century and continues to typify the refined tastes and courtly traditions of antebellum life.

Parlange Plantation has been designated a National Historic Landmark and is listed on the National Register of Historic Places.

Open by appointment. Call (225) 638-8410.

La. Hwy. 1, five miles south of New Roads, along False River.

Parlange Plantation

La Maison DesFossé

(OPEN TO PUBLIC)

Early records and exhaustive research indicate that the original house was built about 1790. In 1850, Dr. Jules Charles DesFossé purchased the "land and improvements" and began extensive renovations to change the appearance to suit his more Anglo-Saxon taste. The house today is a fine example of a mid-19th-century planter's home. A native of Orléans, France, Dr. DesFossé, whose ancestors were chemists, became a prominent dentist in the Mansura area and also served as the town's second mayor.

The simple one-and-a-half-story house reflects the typical construction of the period—bousillage entre poteaux, dried mud between posts. The exterior walls are covered with beaded boarding, and inside are some fine faux finishes.

Restoration of this historic home was directed by La Commission Des Avoyelles, with the assistance of other organizations and individuals.

Open Wednesday-Friday 8:30-3. Call Mansura Town Hall at (318) 964-2152 or the caretaker at (318) 359-3581.

L'Eglise St., Mansura, next to the Cochon de Lait Center and Town Hall, just off La. Hwy. 1.

La Maison DesFossé

TOUR 10

Baton Rouge to St. Francisville

Linwood Plantation

Built by Albert G. Carter between 1838 and 1848, this large two-story plantation home remained in the Carter family until 1910, when it was purchased by the Dougherty family for a home and dairy.

It has four Doric columns across the front, and galleries on both upper and lower floors.

During the Civil War, Union troops used Linwood as a hospital. Sarah Dawson Morgan, author of *A Confederate Girl's Diary*, stayed at Linwood from August 1862 until April 1863. In her diary, she describes the terrifying bombardment of nearby Port Hudson, which began during her stay at Linwood and would turn into the longest and bloodiest siege of the war.

Linwood is listed on the National Register of Historic Places.

Private.

One mile off Old U.S. Hwy. 61, near Jackson.

The Browse

This home was constructed on a section of Troy Plantation, an original Spanish land grant to Isaac Johnson. Johnson was a partner of John Mills, the founder of St. Francisville. The house has always been noted for the extensive gardens surrounding it.

Private.

La. Hwy. 965, south of St. Francisville.

Oakley Plantation/Audubon State Historic Site
(OPEN TO PUBLIC)

Oakley is best known as the plantation where John James Audubon first became acquainted with the abundant wildlife of the Feliciana countryside. No place in Louisiana is richer in memories of the artist-naturalist.

The plantation is now the Audubon State Historic Site, a hundred-acre forested tract centered by the wonderful West Indies-style Oakley House. Built around 1806 and ideally suited to its wooded surroundings, the house has raised living floors above a brick basement, exterior stairs, double jalousied galleries to admit cooling breezes, and fine wooden Adam fireplace mantels. The home's furnishings are fine pieces of the late Federal period, during which the artist was in residence as tutor for the young daughter of the family.

The plantation was established in the late 1790s by Ruffin Gray, whose widow wed James Pirrie. It was the Pirries' beautiful young daughter Eliza, "belle of the Felicianas," who was Audubon's 16-year-old pupil, to be schooled in drawing and dancing, scholastic subjects, and the social arts. The artist was to receive payment of $60 a month and have half of each day free to roam the woods. Among the verdant woodlands and wealth of birdlife, he would paint a number of his famous bird studies here in 1821.

Oakley Plantation

The large detached plantation kitchen building also contains a weaving room and wash room, and the plantation barn is full of vintage implements. Several slave cabins and restored kitchen gardens offer additional insight into antebellum plantation life.

Oakley is listed on the National Register of Historic Places. Open for tours daily 9-5; closed major holidays. Picnic pavilion; hiking trail. Living-history demonstrations most weekends. Call (225) 635-3739. Online www.lastateparks.com. 11788 La. Hwy. 965, south of St. Francisville.

St. Francisville to Laurel Hill

Propinquity

Propinquity is a solid brick townhouse constructed in 1809 by John H. Mills, who founded Bayou Sara. The structure faithfully reflects the Spanish colonial period in the history of the Felicianas.

In the 1820s a German merchant operated it as a store, and it was patronized by the artist John James Audubon and his wife.

Propinquity is listed on the National Register of Historic Places. Private.

9780 Royal St., St. Francisville.

Virginia

Built in 1817 by a Philadelphia merchant, the structure was initially used to house a store. Attractive additions were made in 1826 and also in 1855, when the Victorian two-story wing was constructed by attorney Lorenzo Brewer, who was later killed in a steamboat explosion.

Virginia is in St. Francisville's extensive National Register Historic District. Private.

9838 Royal St., St. Francisville.

Camilla Leake Barrow House

One of the oldest homes in St. Francisville and within the city's National Register Historic District, the Camilla Leake Barrow House was in the Leake family for more than 100 years. The family's connection began with the home in 1866, when young W. W. Leake began to read law with the resident attorney.

The two-story section was begun around 1809 and was soon occupied by town postmaster Amos Webb. The cottage section was added about 1858 by J. Hunter Collins for use as a law office.

Overnight accommodations. Call (225) 635-4791. Online www.topteninn.com.

Corner of Johnson and Royal St., St. Francisville.

Rosedown Plantation State Historic Site

Rosedown Plantation State Historic Site

(OPEN TO PUBLIC)

A graceful two-story structure with wings of cement-covered brick and a wide front veranda supported by six columns, Rosedown was built in 1835 by wealthy planter Daniel Turnbull for his wife, Martha Barrow. The impressive main house represents a harmonious blending of Louisiana plantation, Georgian, and classic styles of architecture.

It is approached by a magnificent oak avenue and is surrounded by 28 acres of formal gardens filled with heirloom plants. Martha Turnbull was inspired by the great formal gardens of France and Italy seen on her European honeymoon and kept a daily diary of her Rosedown gardens as she became one of the first to import camellias, azaleas, and other exotic plantings to the south.

Part of Rosedown's property was a Spanish land grant made in 1789 to John Mills, the founder of Bayou Sara. Daniel Turnbull purchased additional land to form a cotton plantation of more than 3,000 acres.

The Office of State Parks now preserves 371 acres surrounding the house, as well as 13 historic dependencies, including the detached open-hearth kitchen and tiny doctor's office.

Rosedown remained in the original family until it was purchased in the 1950s by Texas preservationist Catherine Fondren Underwood, who directed the meticulous 10-year restoration of house and gardens that turned Rosedown into one of America's most distinguished showplaces.

Rosedown Plantation is a National Historic Landmark and is listed on the National Register of Historic Places.

Open daily 9-5, last tour begins at 4; closed major holidays. Entrance fee. Living-history demonstrations most weekends. Weddings and events. Call (225) 635-3332. Online www.crt.state.la.us/parks/irosedown.aspx. 12501 La. Hwy. 10 at U.S. Hwy. 61, St. Francisville.

The Myrtles

The Myrtles Plantation
(OPEN TO PUBLIC)

One and a half stories tall with wide, 110-foot-long verandas ornamented with elaborate iron grillwork, this house is set in a grove of crepe myrtles and towering live oaks. Built about 1796 by Gen. David Bradford, leader of the Whiskey Rebellion, the house was enlarged and embellished by succeeding owners. Its elaborate interior plaster friezes and lacy iron railings on the galleries are especially notable features.

The Myrtles is billed as "One of America's Most Haunted Homes," and popular weekend mystery tours recount various gruesome deaths and murders said to have taken place here over the years.

The Myrtles is listed on the National Register of Historic Places.

Open daily 9-5. Overnight accommodations. Weddings and special events. Restaurant. Entrance fee. Call (225) 635-6277. Online www.myrtlesplantation.com.

7747 U.S. Hwy. 61, St. Francisville.

Butler Greenwood Plantation

Butler Greenwood Plantation
(OPEN TO PUBLIC)

Butler Greenwood dates from the 1790s and is still owned and occupied by direct descendents of the builder, Samuel Flower, the first doctor in the area and, like most of the early settlers here, of English descent. His daughter wed Judge George Mathews, longtime chief justice of the state supreme court after Louisiana became a state in 1812.

The plantation cash crops were indigo and then cotton. The main house is a raised, rambling English-style two-story structure of cypress, surrounded by 19th-century gardens and a huge grove of live oaks. The detached kitchen of slave-made brick dates from 1796 and shows distinct Spanish architectural influence, as this area remained under Spanish control until 1810.

The home contains one of the finest original formal Victorian parlors in the state, complete with a 12-piece set of rosewood furniture, Belgian carpeting, huge gilded French pier mirrors, and oil portraits of many generations of the same family.

Butler Greenwood Plantation is listed on the National Register of Historic Places.

Open daily 9-5. Overnight accommodations. Call (225) 635-6312. Online www.butlergreenwood.com.

8345 U.S. Hwy. 61, 3 miles north of St. Francisville.

Catalpa Plantation

Catalpa Plantation
(OPEN BY APPOINTMENT)

This charming Victorian cottage was built in 1885 on one of the early antebellum home sites in Louisiana. The large cotton and sugarcane plantation was begun in the 1790s by William J. Fort, whose descendents married into the Turnbull/Bowman family of nearby Rosedown Plantation. The original home here burned.

Noteworthy features include beautiful antique furnishings and fine oil portraits, many from Rosedown.

The rare elliptical entrance drive is lined with a double-horseshoe alley of live oaks hung with Spanish moss, and informal plantings throughout the grounds feature ancient hydrangeas, camellias, and azaleas. The indigo beds near the house are lined with enormous pink conch shells, and in antebellum days there was a servant whose sole job was to keep the shells polished and gleaming.

Open by appointment. Entrance fee. Call (225) 635-3372. Online www.catalpaplantation.com.

U.S. Hwy. 61, five miles north of St. Francisville.

The Cottage Plantation

The Cottage Plantation
(OPEN TO PUBLIC)

This low, rambling, two-story house with an exceptionally long front gallery is, in reality, a series of buildings erected between 1795 and 1859, enlarging an original structure in the Spanish tradition. It is built completely of virgin cypress, except for its massive 16-foot-by-16-foot sills of blue poplar. Twelve posts support the gabled roof.

The original land grant was signed by Baron de Carondelet in 1795. The Cottage was purchased in 1811 by Judge Thomas Butler, who practiced law in the Florida Parishes and represented the area in the U.S. Congress. Gen. Andrew Jackson was a visitor here in 1815, en route to Natchez after his victory in the Battle of New Orleans. Tradition states that he and his large group of officers, including chief of staff Gen. Robert Butler, brother of the host, and seven other Butlers, so overcrowded the accommodations that the host had to sleep in the pantry.

"The Fighting Butlers" loom large in American history. Col. Thomas Butler (father of the judge) was one of five brothers in the Revolutionary army commended for gallantry by Washington. Another of the five, Maj.

Gen. Richard B. Butler, placed the American flag on the British works at Yorktown after Cornwallis surrendered. Capt. Richard Butler, a cousin of the judge, owned Ormond Plantation.

The Cottage is surrounded by many of the original plantation outbuildings, including slave quarters, law office, milk house, detached kitchen, carriage house, smokehouse, commissary, and tack room. Inside, among many original furnishings are mementoes of a banquet given for the Grand Duke Alexis of Russia in 1872. The Cottage is listed on the National Register of Historic Places. Open daily 9:30-4:30; closed holidays. Entrance fee. Overnight accommodations. Call (225) 635-3674. Online www.cottageplantation.com. 10528 Cottage Ln. off U.S. Hwy. 61, five miles north of St. Francisville.

Rosale Plantation

This plantation was originally called "Egypt" when it was established by Alexander Stirling on a Spanish land grant in 1795. It was known as "China Lodge" when David Barrow purchased it in 1845, five years before he built Afton Villa. Rosale was given its present name by Barrow's daughter Mary and her husband, Robert Hilliard Barrow, when they received it as a wedding gift.

In 1810, this plantation was the site of the first meeting of Feliciana planters determined to rid their lands of Spanish rule and establish the carefully planned but short-lived free Republic of West Florida. During its occupancy by Barrow descendant Gen. Robert Barrow, retired commandant of the U.S. Marine Corps, Rosale was beautifully restored and it is now listed on the National Register of Historic Places.

Private.

U.S. Hwy. 61, about seven miles north of St. Francisville.

Wakefield Plantation

Established between 1834 and 1836 by Lewis Stirling, son of Rosale's Alexander Stirling, Wakefield Plantation's main house was a two-and-a-half-story columned structure of imposing proportions. It was named after Oliver Goldsmith's novel, *The Vicar of Wakefield*.

Lewis Stirling was one of the outstanding figures in the Florida Parishes' rebellion against Spain, and it was he who urged the planters to hold the initial meeting at Egypt (Rosale), which blossomed into open revolt and then independence.

Stirling willed the property to his heirs, and in an unusual estate settlement the house was physically divided into three parts. Two heirs retained the first-floor section now occupying the present site; the upper floor and attic were removed in 1877 and rebuilt elsewhere as cottages. They have since burned.

Wakefield is listed on the National Register of Historic Places.

Private.

U.S. Hwy. 61, about eight miles north of St. Francisville.

Tanglewild Plantation

Tanglewild Plantation was established in the early 1800s by members of the Hamilton family, whose descendents still retain ownership of the extensive property.

The original home on the plantation burned and was replaced in the early 1900s.

Private.

U.S. Hwy. 61, nine miles north of St. Francisville near Laurel Hill.

Laurel Hill Plantation

Built in the 1820s on a 216-acre Spanish land grant, Laurel Hill was the home of the Argue family. The plantation was acquired in 1833 by Judge Edward McGehee, who founded the West Feliciana-Woodville railroad, an early standard gauge line hauling cotton from the plantations of southwest Mississippi and the Felicianas to the Mississippi River at Bayou Sara below St. Francisville.

The large Carolina-I home is constructed of hand-hewn logs covered with clapboard. The lower gallery has six square wooden columns; the upper gallery is smaller and partly enclosed.

Just beyond Laurel Hill is the tiny Gothic St. John's Episcopal Church, erected in 1873 and still in use.

Laurel Hill is listed on the National Register of Historic Places.

Private.

Harris-Corner Rd. off U.S. Hwy. 61, Laurel Hill.

TOUR 10B

St. Francisville to Retreat

Highland Plantation

This historic two-story home of cypress, blue poplar, and hand-burned brick was built by William Barrow in 1804 along Little Bayou Sara on a 3,600-acre Spanish land grant. Barrow's widowed mother, Olivia Ruffin Barrow, had journeyed by covered wagon and riverboat with grown children to establish a dynasty in early Feliciana, and Highland was the first of many fine homes this family would build.

The house, with the exception of the window blinds, was constructed solely of materials built, finished, or hand-wrought on the plantation by slave labor. The shutters were made in Cincinnati, Ohio, from cypress logs cut on the plantation.

Originally called Locust Ridge, the plantation was renamed Highland to honor a new variety of cotton grown there by Barrow's son Bennett, who also planted 150 live oaks around the house in 1832 and whose memoirs comprise the fascinating book *Plantation Life in the Florida Parishes: 1836-1846*.

Highland contains superior cabinetwork and hand-carved wainscoting as well as door and window frames. Its most unusual feature is a Palladian window on the upper floor.

Highland Plantation is listed on the National Register of Historic Places.

Private.

8386 Highland Rd., off La. Hwy. 66, Weyanoke.

Woodland

Woodland

This well-preserved raised cottage with six large round columns crossing the galleries was built in 1849 with a main story of wood over a raised brick basement. A covered carriageway originally passed through the lower floor.

Woodland was built near Washington on the other side of the Mississippi River but had connections to West Feliciana and St. Francisville through its builder and earliest occupants. In the opening years of the 21st century, David Norwood, Barrow descendent, undertook the enormous task of moving the entire house to family property near Highland Plantation, where it seems right at home in that pastoral setting.

Private.

Highland Rd., off La. Hwy. 66, Weyanoke.

Greenwood Plantation

Greenwood Plantation
(OPEN TO PUBLIC)

Enormous Greenwood was built in 1830 by William Ruffin Barrow and designed by noted architect James Hammon Coulter. Twenty-eight Doric pillars more than 30 feet high encircled the house. The woodwork was fashioned from native cypress logs, and the home was one of the South's finest examples of Greek Revival architecture. It centered a 12,000-acre cotton plantation

In 1915, the property was purchased by Frank and Naomi Fisher Percy, who restored and refurnished the home and opened it to the public for tours and to Hollywood for movie-making. As the elderly Percys enjoyed a visit from a grandson on August 1, 1960, lightning struck the northeast corner of the house. The entire structure burned to the ground, leaving only the massive columns standing, along with some chimneys.

In 1968, Walton J. Barnes and his son, Richard, purchased the site and determined to make the huge commitment to rebuild the plantation house as close to the original as possible. Once again the setting is popular with tourists and filmmakers.

Open daily 9-5, March 1-October 31; open daily 10-4, November 1-February 28; closed major holidays. Entrance fee. Overnight accommodations. Weddings and special events. Call (225) 655-4475. Online www.greenwoodplantation.com.

6838 Highland Rd., near La. Hwy. 66-La. Hwy. 968 intersection, Weyanoke.

Ellerslie Plantation

A tall, square, plastered-brick structure, the home is surrounded by wide double galleries. Immense Doric columns rise from the lower-floor gallery up to the high hip roof.

Designed by James Hammon Coulter, who also designed nearby Greenwood, Ellerslie was built in 1835 by Judge William C. Wade, a wealthy Carolinian. For several generations it has been occupied by the Percy family; the young ladies of the early generations were pupils of Audubon.

Built on a high bluff overlooking Little Bayou Sara, Ellerslie was originally a cotton and sugarcane plantation, then a cattle ranch. The home has a haunting beauty and is ranked as one of the two most perfect examples of antebellum Greek Revival architecture in the Deep South.

Private.

La. Hwy. 968, one mile off La. Hwy. 66, Weyanoke.

Rosebank Plantation

Constructed of cypress over a high brick basement, this house was said to have operated as an old Spanish inn during the closing years of the 1700s. It was run by John O'Connor, who served as *alcalde* (Spanish magistrate) of the district. The house has long galleries across the front that are supported by round brick Doric columns. The lower floor is of brick, and the upper floors are accessed by exterior stairs. It was later owned by the Barrow family. Rosebank is listed on the National Register of Historic Places.
Private.
La. Hwy. 66, Weyanoke.

Live Oak Plantation

Dating from the early 1800s, Live Oak Plantation house is a two-story structure set flush on the ground, its downstairs walls a full foot thick. It has four squat stucco-covered brick pillars supporting the second-floor gallery, which is reached by exterior stairs. Built by Cyrus Ratliff, during one period it was owned by a member of the Barrow family. It has been used as apothecary shop, schoolhouse, post office, and gracious home, now beautifully restored by the Turner family, long active in historic preservation.
Live Oak is listed on the National Register of Historic Places.
Private.
11365 Tunica Tr. (La. Hwy. 66), Weyanoke.

Weyanoke Plantation

A two-story frame house with gabled roof and plastered front, Weyanoke housed a little school where the wife of John James Audubon tutored children of the family and neighboring plantations in the 1820s.
Originally a log cabin, the house had an upper story added in 1856 by Maj. John Towles. Audubon certainly was a frequent visitor and may have used a subject from the plantation for his *Wild Turkey* painting.
Weyanoke Plantation is listed on the National Register of Historic Places.
Private.
Hollywood Rd., off La. Hwy. 66, Weyanoke.

Retreat Plantation

Established in the early 1850s by Capt. Clarence Mulford, this plantation was originally called Soldier's Retreat.
It is situated on a bluff overlooking Little Bayou Sara and stands in a grove of moss-hung live oak trees. The dormered roof is supported by four round stucco-covered brick columns.
Private.
On La. Hwy. 66, at Retreat.

TOUR 10C

St. Francisville to Clinton

Locust Grove State Historic Site
(OPEN TO PUBLIC)
Established on a Spanish land grant, Locust Grove was the plantation home of the Luther L. Smiths. Mrs. Smith, the former Anna Eliza Davis, was the sister of Jefferson Davis, president of the Confederacy.

The home was destroyed by fire. Now, the center of interest on the grounds is a small, shaded cemetery of only a few dozen graves. The Smiths are buried here, as is Sarah Knox Taylor Davis, daughter of Zachary Taylor and the first wife of Jefferson Davis. She died of malaria in 1835 at age 21, only three months after she and Davis married. Another grave is that of Gen. Eleazer W. Ripley, hero of the Battle of Lundy's Lane, near Niagara Falls, in the War of 1812.

Open daily 9-5; closed holidays. Periodic grave-rubbing demonstrations. Call (225) 635-3789. Online www.crt.state.la.us/parks/ilocust.aspx.

Bains-Ristroph Rd., off La. Hwy. 10, east of St. Francisville.

Wildwood
Wildwood, once the summer home of the Albert Soule family of New Orleans, is a nine-bedroom, three-story farmhouse dating from 1915.

Situated on a 450-acre plantation near Rosedown, the home lay in disrepair for many years until 1958, when it was beautifully restored by the Conrad McVeas.

Wildwood is listed on the National Register of Historic Places.

Private.

La. Hwy. 10, east of St. Francisville.

Roseneath

Roseneath

Roseneath dates to 1830, and at one time it served as a school for the children of Jackson, which was once known as the Athens of the South for its large number of antebellum educational institutions and many columned structures. This three-story Greek Revival home features huge fluted Doric columns and a graceful, winding interior stairway.

For many years it was the home of two sisters, "Miss Bea" Johnston and "Miss Dud" Acosta, local historians and avid preservationists who were the beloved repositories of all the memories every small town should cherish: the Indian scalpings, the bride-to-be swept out of the window by a cyclone, the visit of town namesake Gen. Andrew Jackson, and all the other stories of the city's heritage.

Roseneath is listed on the National Register of Historic Places.

Private.

1662 Erin St. at Bank St., Jackson.

Milbank

Milbank
(OPEN TO PUBLIC)

This classic Greek Revival structure with 30-foot Doric columns was built between 1825 and 1836. It is the oldest commercial structure in town, and its site was once owned by the founders of the town of Jackson, John Horton and James Ficklin.

A two-story home with double galleries, it has served a number of uses over the years. Originally the early banking house for the Clinton-Port Hudson Railroad, it has been a private residence, public assembly hall, hotel, dancehall, apothecary shop, millinery, and newspaper publishing house. During the Civil War, Union soldiers used the structure as troop barracks.

Open for tours by appointment. Entrance fee. Overnight accommodations. Weddings and special events. Call (225) 634-5901. Online www.milbankbandb.com.

3045 Bank St., one block off La. Hwy. 10, Jackson.

Asphodel Plantation

A fine example of the Greek Revival style, Asphodel was built between 1820 and 1833 by Benjamin Kendrick, whose daughter was a pupil of John James Audubon. It consists of a raised central structure and two identical wings of brick covered with a smooth plaster made by slaves using sand from a nearby creek. A wide gallery crosses the front of the main building, and six white Doric columns support the gabled roof, which has two dormer windows. Each wing is a miniature of the central building with a small porch.

Used during the filming of *The Long Hot Summer*, starring Joanne Woodward, Paul Newman, and Orson Welles, Asphodel is listed on the National Register of Historic Places.

Private.

La. Hwy. 68, near Jackson.

Lakeview/Fairview

The house is a two-story frame structure with a front gallery crossing its entire length. Built in the 1840s by William East, Lakeview was beautifully restored by Dr. and Mrs. Kernan Irwin. Of particular interest is the old brick kitchen, which is still in its original condition.

Private.

La. Hwy. 963, between Gurley and Clinton.

Glencoe Plantation

This exuberant structure has been called the finest example of Queen Anne Victorian architecture in the state. The house was built in 1897 by Robert Thompson, Sr., and is a compendium of architectural styles. When it burned in 1903, it was immediately rebuilt exactly as it had been.

Will Rogers, Sr., and Tom Mix were frequent visitors on cattle-buying trips to Thompson Plantation, as the place was once known.

Glencoe is listed on the National Register of Historic Places.

Private.

9616 La. Hwy. 68, Jackson.

Oakland Plantation

Built in 1827 by Judge Thomas W. Scott of South Carolina, this Carolina-I home shows obvious architectural influences of his native state. Raised on brick pillars interspaced with lattice, the house has a wide front gallery running its entire length. Above the gallery's slanting roof is a line of shutters. The eaves are high and the roof is steep. Two large double doors, measuring almost eight feet across, highlight the front entrance. Features of the house include woodwork of the Federal period, beaded boards for walls, plank ceilings, and molded Adam mantels. A spacious corridor runs through the house. The two-story original brick kitchen/dining room, detached from the main house, remains in use.

Oakland is listed on the National Register of Historic Places.
Private.
La. Hwy. 963, eight miles west of Clinton, near Gurley.

The Shades

This two-story red brick home was built by Alexander Scott about 1808 on a land grant. Bordering the brick walk leading to the entrance is tall boxwood, and ivy twines its way around the thick porch columns. The kitchen, a main wing of the home, is built flush with the ground, its porches enclosed by narrow columns.

The late Miss Eva Scott, great-granddaughter of the original builder, lived at the Shades until her death and was widely known for her interesting collection of almost 1,000 old bells.

The Shades is listed on the National Register of Historic Places.
Private.
La. Hwy. 952, about three miles west of Wilson.

Hickory Hill

Built about 1810 by David McCants of South Carolina, Hickory Hill is a tall, narrow structure of red brick. Four white plastered-brick Doric columns rise to the fanlighted pediment of the front facade. The two outer columns are square and the inner two round. A brick wall encloses the ends of both upper and lower galleries.

During the Civil War, the 15-year-old son of the family, home on furlough, was forced to conceal himself in a childhood hiding place under the attic steps to avoid capture by Union troops searching the house.
Private.
La. Hwy. 952, about one mile past the Shades.

Richland

One of the most impressive homes in the Felicianas, Richland was built by Elias Norwood between 1820 and 1830 for his bride, Katherine Chandler, of South Carolina.

Construction is of painted brick with four Doric columns at the front portico. The brick was made from native clay by slave labor. Inside, an exquisite unsupported spiral stairway soars to the third floor, and beautiful Italian marble mantels adorn each room on the lower floor.

Richland is listed on the National Register of Historic Places.
Private.
La. Hwy. 422, five miles east of Norwood.

Bonnie Burn

Bonnie Burn was built prior to 1847 by James Holmes. It was purchased in 1868 by J. G. Kilbourne, a Clinton lawyer and Confederate army captain.

Bonnie Burn (Scottish for the "pretty creek," which flows nearby) was fired upon by Federal troops, and fragments of a Confederate cannon may be seen.
Private.
Off La. Hwy. 10, in Clinton.

Brame-Bennett House

Built in 1840, this house is a fine small example of Greek Revival architecture. Six Doric columns in front support the pediment, which contains a unique sliding fan-shaped window.

The delicacy of the ornamentation above the doorways and windows is of particular interest, as is the graceful winding stairway in the hall. The restored slave quarters and kitchen are in back of the house, as is the circular-shaped well shed, which is also of the Greek Revival style of architecture.

The house is the only residence in East Feliciana Parish chosen for a permanent graphic record in the Library of Congress by the Historic American Buildings Survey. The Brame-Bennett House is listed on the National Register of Historic Places.
Private.
La. Hwy. 67, Clinton.

Lane Plantation

Constructed circa 1825 by the Weston family, the Lane Plantation house reflects a distinctive South Carolina architectural influence. Of clapboard construction atop brick pillars, the home also includes English country influences.

Purchased by William Allen Lane in 1830, the home stands just as it did originally, except for the addition of a kitchen wing on the west and a master bedroom wing on the east. The doors and interior walls are of plank. Original glass panes remain in many windows.

Family mementoes kept here include the peg leg of James Tyson Lane, which he wore after losing a leg in the Civil War.

Lane Plantation is listed on the National Register of Historic Places.

Private.

Off La. Hwy. 955, eight miles southwest of Clinton.

Avondale Plantation

Built around 1830 by David and Elizabeth d'Armond, this Greek Revival raised cottage was moved to its present location in 1981 and restored to its original beauty.

Avondale Plantation is listed on the National Register of Historic Places.

Private.

Off La. Hwy. 10, east of Clinton.

Stonehenge

Built on a hillside and now shaded by large live oak trees, Stonehenge dates from 1837. Judge Lafayette Saunders built this imposing Greek Revival home as well as the magnificent 1840 East Feliciana Courthouse and a law office on Clinton's lovely Lawyer's Row.

A unique feature of the interior of the home is a wooden lattice screen dividing the front and back hall.

Private.

La. Hwy. 67, Clinton.

Plovanich Place

Plovanich Place was rebuilt from the Hunter Brothers Store (circa 1870) of Waterproof, Louisiana, with the original red cypress wood and unusual wood siding simulating stone.

It is said that Huey P. Long made his first political speech from the front gallery.

Private.

La. Hwy. 63, south of Clinton (off La. Hwy. 67).

Marston House

Originally built as a bank in 1838, Marston House has lately been used as the headquarters for the East Feliciana Pilgrimage and Garden Club. In 1851, Henry Marston bought the property from the Union Bank of New Orleans and converted the building into a commodious residence. Marston House is listed on the National Register of Historic Places.
Private.
Bank St., Clinton.

Martin Hill

Named for the many purple martins inhabiting the grounds, Martin Hill is a lovely Greek Revival raised cottage dating back to the early 1840s. Heinrich Mayer, a prominent merchant in Clinton, enlarged the home around 1900. The elaborate front doors still show the initial "M" in glass. Among other remarkable features of this home are the interior doors and staircase.
Private.
St. Helena St. (La. Hwy. 10), Clinton.

Old Wall Parsonage

The Reverend Isaac Wall, a Methodist circuit rider, and his wife Mary Winans, daughter of a prominent Methodist clergyman, built the original parsonage in 1840.
The Old Wall Parsonage is listed on the National Register of Historic Places.
Private.
Woodville St., Clinton.

Blairstown

This two-story home, built in 1850 by Samuel Lee, is a fine example of the Greek Revival style of architecture. It was constructed by slave laborers, who cut the timber and made the brick on the property. Horse hair was mixed in with the plaster to bind it more efficiently, and square-shaped nails were used in the construction.
Private.
La. Hwy. 959, at Blairstown, five miles west of La. Hwy. 67.

TOUR 11

Milliken (Ark.-La. line) to Tallulah

Arlington

Arlington is majestically situated in a grove of ancient magnolia, live oak, cypress, cedar, and black walnut trees. The first story of this two-story house is made of brick, the second of cypress; both have wide verandas extending across the front and around the east end of the house. Built about 1841 for Mrs. T. R. Patten, the house was originally a one-story building of cypress. A later owner, Gen. Edward Sparrow, senior senator from Louisiana in the Congress of the Confederacy, raised it and added an understory of brick.

During the Civil War, it was used as headquarters for many Union officers, including James McPherson, James McMillan, and Arthur MacArthur. According to tradition, the house was also used by Gen. Ulysses Grant when he visited Lake Providence.

Listed on the National Register of Historic Places, Arlington stands near Grant's Canal—the forlorn monument to the unsuccessful attempt by that general to build a canal across DeSoto Point to enable his gunboats to avoid the Confederate shore batteries during the siege of Vicksburg in 1863.

Private.

214 Arlington Rd., Lake Providence, across from Grant's Canal.

Crescent Plantation House

A gabled roof and eight square columns supporting a wide gallery are important features of this house. The great front doorway, flanked by French windows that extend almost to the top of the 14-foot ceiling, enters upon a spacious hall. Original brass knobs and door locks are still in use, as are its transoms of stained glass, which were all imported from Europe.

Inside, a spiral stairway with a mahogany railing ascends from the rear of the hall to the second floor. The plastered walls and ceiling ornaments are well preserved.

The original house was constructed about 1832, and the present front section was added in 1855. The home is listed on the National Register of Historic Places.

Private.

U.S. Hwy. 80, four and a half miles east of Tallulah.

TOUR 11A

Tallulah to Marion
(U.S. Hwy. 80, La. Hwy. 33)

Carpenter House

A one-story frame structure set on brick pillars with six square wooden columns and a shingled, gabled roof, Carpenter House was a popular inn on the Vicksburg-Monroe stagecoach line during the 1850s.

According to legend, the house was named for Samuel Carpenter, leader of the infamous Kentucky-Cave-in-Rock Bandits, who was slain near Vidalia, Louisiana, in 1803.

Private.

U.S. Hwy. 80/La. Hwy. 17, Delhi.

D'Anemour-O'Kelly House

Reputed to be the oldest house in Monroe, the one-and-a-half-story frame structure was built about 1790 by M. D'Anemour on land granted to Joseph de la Baume. The newer portions of the home were added in 1870 when Col. Henry O'Kelly purchased and renamed it.

The home has wide galleries and square columns. Built without nails, it is of hand-hewn cypress construction, and its massive cypress doors afforded its early inhabitants protection from attacking Indians and bandits.

Private.

Moved to Horseshoe Lake Rd., off U.S. Hwy. 165, about 12 miles north of Monroe.

Little Red Brick House/Fort Miro

Although not a plantation home, this structure occupies a site near the historic Fort Miro, the original Spanish fort in this area. Built in 1790 by Commandant Jean Filhiol and Lt. Joseph de la Baume of the Ouachita District, Fort Miro was a stockade fortification 190 feet by 140 feet and served as protection against Indians. After the city was renamed Monroe, Fort Miro played a lesser role and the land passed through the hands of several individuals.

The present structure was built in 1840 by Samuel Kirby and operated as the law office of Isaiah Garrett. Previous owners of the land were Dr. C. H. Dabbs, Hypolite Pargoud, and Don Juan Filhiol. The house has been preserved by the Monroe Committee of the National Society of Colonial Dames. For many years it served the famous choir of Ouachita Parish High School, located across the street.
Private.
520 South Grand St., Monroe.

Wooten House

The house is simple in design, one story in height, with six square wooden columns across the long front gallery. From the ceiling hang immense handmade iron hooks, from which jugs filled with water were suspended and swung back and forth by slaves to cool the drinking water.

Built around 1824, Wooten House was once the overseer's home for Lower Pargoud Plantation. Wooten House is listed on the National Register of Historic Places.
Private.
2111 South Grand St., Monroe.

Upper Pargoud

Built in the early 19th century as an overseer's home by Hypolite Pargoud, one of Monroe's first wealthy planters and merchants, this frame two-storied structure is considered to be one of the oldest plantation houses in Ouachita Parish. Its gabled roof is broken by wide three-windowed dormers and supported by classic columns.

About 400 yards north of the plantation house, between the levee and the Ouachita River, is the Pargoud Indian Mound. According to unsupported local legend, the mound is the burial place of Wichita, the beautiful daughter of the Indian chief Ucita. She died after being deserted by a member of a Spanish expedition who had married her in gratitude for saving his life.
Private.
At the end of Island Dr., Monroe.

Layton Castle
(OPEN TO PUBLIC)

Incorporated within the aged brick walls of Layton Castle is part of the old Bry house, built about 1814 by Judge Henry Bry, a Swiss immigrant who became a prominent jurist and statesman in early Ouachita. He purchased 500 acres along the Ouachita River and planted mulberry trees with the intent of raising silkworms on his plantation. Consequently, his property was called Mulberry Grove.

Judge Bry was a close friend of Don Juan (Jean Baptiste) Filhiol and often entertained John James Audubon. He led the delegation that welcomed the steamboat *James Monroe*—the first steamboat to sail up the Mississippi—to Fort Miro in 1819 and renamed the settlement Monroe in honor of the occasion.

Judge Bry's original house was considerably enlarged by his daughter Melinda and her husband, Robert Layton, and by 1910 it had been transformed into the castle of today by Eugenia Stubbs Layton, widow of Judge

Layton Castle

Bry's grandson, whose years of living abroad no doubt influenced the architectural embellishments.

Layton Castle, with its arcaded gallery, turret, and porte-cochere with towering Romanesque columns, has the charm of an old-world manor house, its principal architectural feature a tower worthy of feudal Europe. The old brick-walled Bry cemetery is on the grounds, as well as a wonderful little 18th-century brick wine house that may have housed Judge Bry's silkworms. Some of the mulberry trees he planted are still thriving.

Layton Castle is listed on the National Register of Historic Places.

Open for group tours by appointment. Weddings and events. Call (318) 322-4869.

1113 South Grand St., Monroe.

Huey House

This two-story frame house, set upon pillars of native rock, was built before the Civil War by John Huey. It was also used as an inn on the Monroe-Shreveport stagecoach line.

Private.

U.S. Hwy. 167, just north of Ruston.

Davis House

Located near Lake D'Arbonne, this raised one-story house was built about 1890 by James Wade. The construction is of cypress.

Private.

La. Hwy. 33, D'Arbonne, eight miles south of Farmerville.

Read Home

This charming residence is probably the oldest home in Farmerville.

Private.

801 North Main St., Farmerville.

Edgewood

One of the most spectacular homes in north Louisiana, this 12-room Queen Anne Revival landmark is also known as the Baughman Plantation Home. Built in 1902 by Jefferson Baughman, it is situated on a 3,000-acre stand of timber. The entire front of the rambling structure is galleried. Two staircases, one curved, one straight, provide access. The most distinctive feature, however, is a towering turret at the center. Materials for construction were said to have been transported by wagon from Monroe. The home is listed on the National Register of Historic Places.

Private.

La. Hwy. 2, a mile west of Farmerville.

Hopkins House

This two-story structure with two fireplaces on one side occupies a prominent place in musical history. Ann Porter Harrison, the composer of "In the Gloaming," was employed in 1854 to teach music to the children of the residents, Mr. and Mrs. Elias George. A broken romance, and perhaps the beauty of the home, led her to write the popular song.

Private.

Hopkins Ln., Marion, in northeast Union Parish.

TOUR 11B

Tallulah to Vidalia

Winter Quarters State Historic Site

(OPEN TO PUBLIC)

This one-and-a-half story, 19-room frame house set on high brick pillars was built in 1805 by Job Routh on one of the last Spanish land grants to be given in Louisiana. A gallery with five large square columns fronts the house. Originally a three-room hunting cottage used as "winter quarters," the home was enlarged by Routh's granddaughter and her husband, physician and planter Dr. Haller Nutt, accounting for the combination of architectural styles.

More than 2,000 acres formed the plantation, which included several cotton gins.

During the Civil War, Union soldiers destroyed all 15 of the plantation

Winter Quarters State Historic Site

homes lining the banks of Lake St. Joseph, except Winter Quarters, which was used as a stopping point by Gen. Ulysses S. Grant's troops. Winter Quarters is listed on the National Register of Historic Places. Open daily 9-5; closed major holidays. Entrance fee. Call (318) 467-9750. Online www.crt.state.la.us./parks/iwinter.aspx. 4929 La. Hwy. 608, eight miles southeast of Newellton.

Lakewood

Established in 1854 by Capt. A. C. Watson, commander of Watson's Battery during the Civil War, Lakewood was constructed in the typical architectural style of the period.

When Watson left his home to join Gen. Robert E. Lee, he buried some $20,000 on the grounds of Lakewood, most of which he recovered after he returned. Not until 1928 did a descendent uncover the missing jar containing $5,000.

Lakewood is listed on the National Register of Historic Places. Private.
Lake Bruin Rd., in the vicinity of Lake Bruin.

Bondurant House

This one-story house was originally the second story of Pleasant View, a plantation built in 1852 and moved back from the river in the 1880s.

The house was shelled during the Civil War, during which Mrs. Bondurant had more than 100 bales of cotton burned to keep them from falling into the hands of the Union forces.

When the house was moved, cannonballs were found lodged in the timbers. Bullet holes can yet be seen in the front door and the low half-doors that open on French windows.
Private.
Second St., St. Joseph.

Davidson

This elegant house was built around an original log dwelling about 1850 by Joseph Moore, an early Louisiana planter, for his daughter, Mrs. Carrie Moore Davidson. The home contains many original family furnishings.
Private.
St. Joseph.

TOUR 11C

Monroe to Columbia (U.S. Hwy. 165)

Whitehall Plantation House
This Greek Revival home predates the Civil War and is listed on the National Register of Historic Places.
Private.
Buckhorn Bend Rd., Monroe.

Filhiol House
Jean Baptiste (or Don Juan Bautista) Filhiol was the commandant of Fort Miro, Poste des Washitas (Ouachita Post), and founder of the city of Monroe. Don Juan left many descendents in the area. One, his grandson John B. Filhiol, was a wealthy planter who built a one-story frame house called the Filhiol House in 1855. Its lumber was milled from nearby woods, and its hinges and locks were wrought in the plantation's own blacksmith shop.

The inside woodwork was carefully joined with wooden pegs, and the large smoothed and painted rafters eliminated the need for a finished ceiling in the front room. There were square cypress pillars across the front porch, and a fanlight above the entrance door.

The dining room was designed after the dining salon of an old river packet, but when additions were made to the original house, Filhiol imported a French cabinetmaker to give the interior an authentic French look. This house was south of Monroe near Buckhorn Bend on the Ouachita River.

Another Filhiol House, this one in Monroe itself and listed on the National Register of Historic Places, was built in the late 1800s for Roland M. Filhiol, Don Juan's great-grandson, himself a wealthy planter and businessman. This one-and-a-half-story frame house is of the Queen Anne Revival style but has extensive Eastlake influence in its ornamentation both inside and out.
Private.
111 Stone Ave., Monroe.

Synope

This raised Creole cottage has graced the Ouachita River area for nearly two centuries. The interior features four fireplaces and 12-foot-high ceilings. Situated on a 1,500-acre plantation, it is surrounded by a landscaped five-acre garden.

Synope is listed on the National Register of Historic Places.

Private.

U.S. Hwy. 165, 10 miles north of Columbia.

Breston Plantation

The oldest home in Caldwell Parish, this residence may have been constructed as early as the 1790s, although a construction date in the 1830s is more probable. The land on which the one-and-a-half-story, dormered residence stands, on the east bank of the Ouachita River, was bought in 1837 by Jean Baptiste Bres, who had come to Louisiana from France in 1799.

Breston is listed on the National Register of Historic Places.

Private.

Breston Plantation Rd., off La. Hwy. 165 at Riverton, five miles north of Columbia.

Index